8.50p

JENÖ SCHWARZ

A PROMISE REDEEMED

A PROMISE REDEEMED

JENÖ SCHWARZ

Translated from the German by
Sidney Lightman

First published in Germany 1962
English translation © Jenö Schwarz, London 1964

Made and printed in Great Britain
by Butler & Tanner Ltd, Frome and London

CONTENTS

6

THE COLLEGE CLOSES DOWN

IT all began on March 19, 1944. I was just sixteen then and studying under old Chief Rabbi Gross at the Nagykaroly Rabbinical Seminary in Hungary. At least it was Hungary then; today it is part of Rumania.

On that fateful day, all the Seminary's seventy students were gathered round a long table, engrossed in the discourses of our great teacher. Suddenly, somebody flung open the door and, his limbs all a-tremble, shouted: 'The Germans have marched in!'

Our faces grew pale, but nobody dared to leave his place out of respect for our teacher. Although we were all extremely perturbed, we all remained perfectly quiet, our eyes riveted on the rabbi, standing there with his massive volume of the Talmud open before him. He seemed not to have heard the dreadful news, or else to regard it as not being of any particular significance.

Speaking in his usual calm, collected way, he continued with his lecture on the legal view of divorce. Then, he suddenly changed the subject and began to explain a different part of the Talmud.

7

'Our sages tell us in the Talmud,' he said, 'that God has done us Jews a kindness by scattering us among all the nations of the world. Of course, you will all ask, what sort of kindness is it, to disperse a people in such a dreadful way? It appears in fact to be just the opposite of a kindness.'

Then the rabbi told us a parable to explain what the sages had meant. 'A clever general found himself and his army in an extraordinarily difficult situation. He knew that many of his troops would be killed. What did he do, then? He spread them over as great an area as possible, so that the enemy's lethal grenades would not kill the entire army.

'God knew that there would be kings and nations in every generation, who would regard it as their duty to destroy the Jewish people. What did the great general, the Almighty, do? He scattered us among all the nations of the earth, so that no persecutor could ever wipe out the entire Jewish people.

'Isn't that a kindness?' the rabbi cried, raising his voice, and closing his volume of the Talmud as a sign that the lecture was over.

We all leapt up from our benches, but the rabbi gestured with his hand for us all to sit down again. He waited until the room was completely quiet, and then began to speak, softly and with his voice full of anguish:

8

'I think that circumstances make it imperative for you to go home to your parents. The parting will be a painful one for me personally, and I think that the same applies to all of you.

'I just want to give you a tonic to help you on your way—who knows, it might perhaps have been better to say your *via dolorosa*. You cannot obtain this tonic at any chemist's, or buy it in any shop.

'It is a saying of our sages. They teach us: "It is man's duty to thank God for the good that God bestows on him, and also for the evil He causes him." That we should thank God for the good is logical and clear. Indeed, one could say that it is obvious.

'But the question comes immediately to mind, what logical explanation can there be for giving thanks for the evil also? This is explained elsewhere in the Talmud, where the following story is told:

'A man wanted to travel abroad and had already bought his ticket. However, as he was hurrying towards the ship, he slipped and broke his leg. He cursed God for having caused this to happen to him. A short time afterwards, he heard that the ship on which he was to have travelled had sunk.

'Then he said: "Praise be to God's name that He caused me to break my leg and thus saved me from death." From this you can see that many happenings which we regard as evil and saddening, in fact bring

9

good happenings in their train. Only, we do not understand the good that is hidden within them, for we are but as small children compared with God.

'When somebody makes you take some foul-tasting medicine in order to make you better, you regard it as a bad deed committed against yourselves, because you do not understand its deeper significance. Our sages are right, when they say that it is man's duty to thank God for both good and evil.

'It could also be expressed in this way: It is man's duty to thank God for everything that happens, for therein is God's mercy hidden.'

The old rabbi closed his eyes and raised his hands in blessing. He blessed us gently. Only his lips moved, and tears poured from his closed eyes.

One by one, we went up to him and kissed his hand, while he stood there in silence and looked at every one of us in sorrow. Then we all hurried to our lodgings, packed our things and made for the railway station as fast as we could.

I still owed last month's rent, and what little money I had with me would barely cover the cost of my journey home. My old landlord would be back soon. In fact I could already hear his heavy footsteps.

He had something important, something urgent, to tell me. It must be something drastic, if he could not wait to speak until he had entered the house. He stopped on the narrow staircase outside the window six feet up in the wall of my room.

It was impossible to see anything clearly through it because it was glazed with frosted glass, although one could tell whether the light was on or off. The light was on. It was always on when I was in my room, even in broad daylight, because the little dormer window was quite inadequate to dissipate its twilight gloom.

Mr Roth pressed his long, narrow face, with its silver-grey, Vandyke beard, between the bars of the lattice across the window which was nearly eaten away with rust. I saw his pointed nose, his extremely wide mouth and half of his dishevelled beard. The rest of his face was outside the lattice, which forced up the broad brim of his hard round hat, so that the lower edge of the crown dug into the gap between his shirt collar and his skin at the back.

Mr Roth tapped on the window with the backs of his trembling hands. Although he could reach the window from the steps, it was right at the top of the wall inside the room. In fact, its upper edge touched the ceiling and one would have had to stand on a chair to reach it. Since there was no chair in the room, the table would have to do. I jumped up onto it and saw the landlord's face through the open window. It had gone almost as grey as his beard. His unusually small cat's eyes, magnified by his glasses, were as wide open as they could ever be and darting wildly from side to side. If it had not been for the lattice, his head would have been shaking backwards and forwards even more violently.

'D-d-d-do you know?' he stammered, taking his head away from the lattice so that he could beat his hands together. 'Oh lord, oh lord, the Germans . . .' The rest of the sentence was lost in a flood of tears as Mr Roth started wailing like a child. He put both arms along the window-ledge and laid his face on them. His hat fell off, revealing his bald head. 'Oh, oh, the Germans, do you know, the Germans!' I did know, of course, but made no sign. I put my hand through the lattice and stroked Mr Roth's bald head.

Mrs Weiss hurried over from next door. She did not ask what the crying was about. Her damp eyes showed that she herself had been crying not very long before. Who was not crying? But she wanted to take the old man in off the street before the crowd of curious children, who had gathered to see what was going on, grew even bigger.

The old man refused to move away from the window. 'Oh lord, the Germans,' he mumbled again. I jumped off the table, raced through the dining-room, seized him by the arm and took him onto the terrace. Close to fainting, Mr Roth slumped down into a dirty grey armchair. His eyes were closed and his body had stopped trembling, but he kept on mumbling: 'The Germans, the Germans!'

I reached for a cloth and held it under the tap. Then I went back to the old man. There was no need for me to undo his shirt buttons, because they had all been torn off. I began to rub his chest with the wet cloth. The old man straightened up, and I stared at him in amazement as he said in a loud firm voice: 'God is with us. He will not desert us!' His voice rose almost to a scream: 'No, no, no, He will not desert us!'

We went inside and sat down at the table. 'Listen,' I began, 'I have to go home.'

'What! And leave me here all alone, at a time like this!' He was a widower, and childless.

'The rabbi said we must.' If the rabbi had said so, then Mr Roth would not dare to contradict. The rabbi's command was God's command.

'The rent, I——'

'Nonsense,' interrupted Mr Roth. 'You've got bigger worries now.' He took out a small key he always carried in his jacket pocket, opened the worm-eaten brown wooden cupboard and took out a small iron cash-box. He had a small fortune—or perhaps a large one—tucked away in it. Mr Roth

13

had little faith in banks. He had already had experience of them in the First World War. The cupboard was safer.

He emptied the box onto the table. 'How foolish people are,' he sighed. 'You work your whole life, you slave, you sweat like a pig, so that you won't be left destitute when you grow old. And what is it all worth now, when your life itself is in danger? Wouldn't I have done better to have bought food for starving children and orphans with it?'

There were still two hours before the train left. I debated whether to go over and see the rabbi. Before I had made up my mind, the rabbi's twelve-year-old son burst in. He took no notice of the old man, but came straight over to me. 'The rabbi would like to talk to you,' he said. Out of respect, he always referred to his father as 'the rabbi', never 'my father'. I took the boy's arm and hurried out of the house with him. A group of bearded men had already gathered at the next street corner and were whispering to each other. They quickly dispersed, because gatherings had been forbidden even before the Germans marched in, and to stand about in a group was still more dangerous now. I saw many similar groups before I reached the rabbi's house.

In the huge courtyard stood more than a hundred people. The atmosphere was like a funeral. I knocked on the door of the small room to which the rabbi retreated for most of the day, so that he could study undisturbed. Nothing could be seen of the walls. They were hidden by piles of books stacked from floor to ceiling all round the room.

There was no answer to my knocking. I walked in quietly, just the same. The rabbi was seated at a desk that looked as if it was six hundred years old, leafing through a thick manuscript. He had not even noticed that someone had come in.

I stood there motionless until he looked up, turning his large, clever eyes on me in surprise. 'It is a good thing you have come. I was just thinking about you,' he exclaimed, pushing a chair towards me. I sat down facing him, and he took my hand in his.

'Thirty years ago,' he began, 'your grandfather and I were at a banquet at the house of my father-in-law, the famous wonder rabbi of Bodrog-Keresztur. Towards three o'clock in the morning, the rabbi's usually jolly face grew serious. He turned to your grandfather and said:

' "You know, Reb Mechul, before the good Lord leads his people back to the Holy Land, the Jews will have to endure the most dreadful sufferings, the worst since they were created. The world will be stained with Jewish blood. I shall not survive to experience these dreadful happenings, but you will have to endure some of them. In this country, they will start with your grandson.

' "I hope that it will happen in this village, where my grave will be. I promise you that I will stand by him to ease his sorrow. I owe you that, Reb Mechul, for you have always been one of those closest to me." With a deep sigh, he added: "Yes, they will be terrible times."

'Who can say,' my teacher continued, 'whether you are not the grandchild my father-in-law spoke of? I advise you to go at once to Bodrog-Keresztur. It is near enough to your home town. Go to my father-in-law's grave, say a prayer there and light some candles. I will give you some to take with you.' The rabbi accompanied me to the door and shook my hand in parting.

THE JOURNEY HOME

A huge crowd was waiting for the train which, it had been announced, would be running an hour late. Half my fellow students were standing on the platform. The rest had already left. Their faces were pale and worried. They beckoned to me, but I did not join them. I had even less taste than usual for empty discussions. All my thoughts were taken up with the secret prophecies of the famous rabbi.

My comrades came over to me. 'What do you say about it? What is going to become of us now?' Chaim Hoffmann, the oldest of the group, asked me.

'Comrades, there is no stronger weapon than joy. The first principle of Chassidism is joy, joy in every situation,' I shouted. 'A Chassidic dance would be more in order here and now than ever before,' I added, and little Chaim began jumping high in the air. After some initial hesitation, everybody joined in. We closed the circle, and the non-Jewish passengers willingly made room for us.

The sound of the Chassidic melody lured the station-master out of his room. At first he did not know how to react to what he saw. Was this the time, and was this the place, when the Germans were on the way, for the Jews to choose for dancing? But the extraordinary scene on the platform aroused his curiosity. Chaim's high-spirited capers, his side-curls swinging wildly from side to side, the station-master found particularly diverting. Riveting his gaze on Chaim, he joined in the clapping of the other non-Jewish spectators, shouting 'Hurrah! Hurrah!' as the melody rang out—'Ve– ta– her– li– be– nu, ve– ta– her– li– be– nu.'

A young Hungarian came out of the waiting-room and threw a baleful glance at the dancers. Then he went back to the waiting-room and came out again with four of his friends. Their hoots and cat-calls found no answering echo in the station. They were in the minority.

They came right up close to the dancing Talmud students, posturing with their feet spread wide and their hands thrust into their trousers pockets. At the tops of their voices, they yelled: 'Long live Hitler and Szalasi! Let's beat up the Jews!'

At that moment the station bell began to ring, signalling the arrival of the train, and this prevented an almost certain riot. Everyone grabbed their luggage.

'That was a beautiful interlude,' remarked Ruben-stein.

18

'The most beautiful ever,' said little Chaim.

We could already see the black smoke cloud thrown out by the whistling iron monster. The wind tried to blow it downwards towards the ground, but failed, and the smoke rolled skywards to join the rest, so that it all merged into a dark, hovering mass. Everyone on the platform knew that this was a sure sign that it would not be long before the train pulled into the platform. Soon we saw the black engine itself, growing momentarily larger, until the train roared into the station.

It was packed to overflowing. Nobody could get off or on. Cases, cardboard boxes and even prams came hurtling through the windows, with people jumping after them. Babes in arms were passed out to the platform to the accompaniment of a babel of shouts—'Ferenc, Pista, the trunk, the child . . .'

I saw a large object fall out of the carriage window. It was not exactly in the best of condition; there were cuts and tears all over it, and shreds of leather hung in tatters from it, but it was still just recognizable as a trunk. It was still good enough to use once as a stepping stone, so I jumped up onto it and lunged at the train window. I landed in the compartment just as the wheels started turning.

It was unfortunate that I should have landed on a lady's lap, a lady, moreover, fully convinced of her high racial standing. Doubly unfortunate was the fact that she was accompanied by her husband.

He thought the insolent Jew deserved a hiding for his behaviour, and hit me hard in the stomach, following the blow with a kick. This I hardly felt, and I did not even hear his unending stream of abuse. The worst of it all was that I could not change my travelling companions. My way was barred by a solid phalanx of broad shoulders and backs.

I wondered to myself whether the punch in the stomach, which I could still feel, had fulfilled the prophecies of the rabbi, who had foretold, thirty years ago: 'Your grandson will be the first one in this country to suffer.' But I soon vanquished this thought. Had not something worse than this little blow in the stomach already happened to me? Only last week, as I had been leaving the Seminary one evening, a sharp stone had hit me on the forehead. It had been a mercy that my eyes had not been damaged. I had lost count of the number of such 'fortunate' incidents—fortunate because they could have turned out so much worse.

The train stopped at Nyiregyhaza. 'All change, all change! Next train tomorrow morning, for technical reasons.' Everybody got out. I stood there in the darkened station, not knowing what to do. The only

light there was came from the waiting-room whenever the door opened for a moment.

The village of Tokay lies twenty miles to the
north of Nyiregyhaza. It is a small place, but everyone has heard of it. Anyone who holds good wine
in esteem will understand this, for when the golden
yellow Tokay wine sparkles in the glasses, it
brightens one's spirits.

I, too, hold the village in high regard, but for
other reasons. There, in Tokay, with its wine-
scented air, I drew my first breath. It was there that
I went to school, and that was why I loved it.

I wandered hither and thither in the dark and
sinister railway station. So did someone else, fourteen-year-old Samuel Friedmann, who came from
Bodrog-Keresztur. When someone opened the
waiting-room door, I happened to be standing in
the path of the dim light and Samuel recognized me
and came over. I found it rather curious, because my
teacher had spoken to me about Bodrog-Keresztur
before I left, and now I had met someone from that
very village.

We already knew each other. There in Bodrog-
Keresztur, another Chassidic rabbi lived, the grandson of that wonder rabbi of whom my teacher had
spoken to me. No longer did thousands of Chassidim
make the pilgrimage to the village at the High Holy

Days, as they once had to see his grandfather, but hundreds still came to receive his blessing.

When I was still a small child, my father and grandfather had taken me with them and I had joined in the many Chassidic dances. Whenever I heard the name Bodrog-Keresztur, it used to bring back wonderful memories of my childhood, but that day, after I had been told about the prophecies of the wonder rabbi, the name began to have a mysterious sound in my ears.

Where to sleep that night? As we were discussing the matter, a man with a beard noticed us. He did not actually see us, because the station was totally blacked-out. There was a war on, and we were not far from the fighting. But he heard us speaking Yiddish, and Yiddish-speakers belong together, especially at such a time. He walked towards our voices and bumped into us.

He told us that his daughter had not arrived when expected, and there would be no more trains now till the next day. Mr Cohen was worried about his daughter's non-arrival, and about many other things too. We were also worried—about where we were going to sleep. Mr Cohen came to the rescue.

The three of us left the station together. We could not see a thing, but Mr Cohen knew every stick and stone and guided us firmly to our goal. He felt his way along the walls of the houses with his right hand and gave Samuel his left. Since Samuel was holding his wordly possessions in his left hand, I held him by the collar.

When we reached Mr Cohen's house, we saw Mrs Cohen. She was standing there with her mouth hanging open and her eyes staring. Her whole face was distorted with fear. Samuel and I thought that this was on account of her daughter. So did Mr Cohen. But she asked quite a different question: 'Are the Germans already here?' None of us was in a position to answer her. In fact, the Germans had not yet arrived in the town. They were in control of Budapest and were fanning out from the capital towards the rest of the country.

Meanwhile, Samuel and I felt happy. We blessed Providence for having sent us a guardian angel in the shape of Mr Cohen. And when he went into a neighbouring room, a weight fell from his heart too, for there sat his missing daughter, drinking coffee. Or perhaps it was tea. It was certainly not milk. Not that the cows were on strike. They do not concern themselves with politics, nor do they make wage demands. The milk they produced, however, was simply not to be had. It had been dried and powdered and sent out to the troops, together with the rest of the munitions they needed.

Up to the day before, babies at least had received a small ration, but now even they did not get any, unless they were Aryan babies. Non-Aryan babies did not need milk any more!

It was a friendly, even pretty room that Mrs Cohen put at our disposal. We were allowed to switch on the light too, because the room had been blacked out by sticking paper over the windows. The bed was soft, the sheets of white linen and everything was comfortable, but I had a feeling that this night was not meant for sleep, although I could not tell why. I just felt that this night was particularly suitable for saying 'Tehillim' (psalms).

Samuel was asleep and snoring loudly. The light did not disturb him. Remarkably enough, Mr Cohen also thought that saying 'Tehillim' was the best way to pass that particular night, and he went on chanting in his wailing voice until morning.

By the time Samuel woke up, I was on the point of dozing off, but did not do so. The train would not wait. I opened the window. Outside it was just growing light. Mr Cohen had finished his 'Tehillim' and fallen asleep—or so we thought. Actually, he was busy in the kitchen, and a little later he brought in two glasses of hot tea. 'Children,' he said, 'after hot tea in the morning, one can face the day without worrying.' I gulped it down eagerly, but Samuel did not want to drink his. He had woken up in a bad mood. 'Are you fasting?' Mr Cohen asked him. 'Did you have a bad dream? Many Jews fast the day after they have had a bad dream.' Samuel shrugged his shoulders and did not answer.

As we stood waiting on the station platform, a long, empty train drew in. We sat down opposite each other on the hard, wooden seats by the window. The rays of the mild spring sun lit up Samuel's delicate, milk-white face, making it look even paler. He looked at me with his greenish-grey eyes, always half-closed but with the sparkle of a fourteen-year-old boy within them. He looked and looked, as if he could not tear his eyes away from me. My head was bent forward slightly, and an open prayer-book lay on my knees. I held the pages with both hands so that the draught would not flutter them. Softly I recited the *Tefilat Haderech* (the prayers for going on a journey). Only when I had finished my prayer and put the slim volume back in my jacket pocket did I pay more attention to my companion. Now I noticed that Samuel's face, which had yesterday seemed so childish and carefree, no longer looked quite as young. In answer to my question he said that he felt all right. 'You look very miserable today, Samuel,' I said. Hesitantly, he explained his failure

25

to obey the highest precept of Chassidism—to be joyful. 'I am not worried about myself,' he replied.

'But——' I interrupted him, a little surprised.

'I'm worried about you,' Samuel said and bowed his head. He looked as if he were searching for something he had dropped on the floor.

'About me?' I asked, even more surprised. 'Why?' Samuel continued to stare at the floor and did not answer. It was obvious that he was undecided whether to answer or not.

At last he looked up and his indecision vanished. He took a deep breath and said: 'I had a dream last night.'

I made a deprecatory gesture with my hands and almost laughed out loud. 'What silly talk. Who pays any attention to a dream?'

Samuel went on even more seriously: 'A dreadful dream, it was.'

I could no longer suppress my laughter. 'A dream is still only a dream, and the more frightening it was the more pleasant one's awakening and the greater the relief. Perhaps you dreamt that I had died? Well, you can see that I'm still alive,' I said banteringly.

'No not that. I saw you lying on the ground, covered with blood, and you were terribly injured.' He sighed deeply. Then I remembered the rabbi's mysterious farewell message of the day before and it was as if a shaft of lightning had struck my soul. Then, when Samuel said: 'It was in my home village of Bodrog-Keresztur,' the words resounded in my head like thunder and my spirit trembled. My blood raced through my veins and I broke out in a drenching sweat. All these reactions took only a second, perhaps less. I put my right hand on my heart as if in pain. But I was not in pain. I merely wanted to press back my heart, which was beating so fiercely that it felt as if it would force its way out of my body.

Next to me sat a wizened old peasant. He had noticed nothing and continued smoking a pipe almost as long as himself. Every time he drew on it there was a glow underneath the ash in the bowl. What he was smoking was supposed to be tobacco, but it was not. There was a war on, and more essential things than tobacco could not be imported. It was obvious, however, that he found the ersatz tobacco he was smoking pretty much to his taste. I also enjoyed it. Not the pipe itself, but the grey smoke curling up from the bowl: He took his time and puffed slowly, the smoke spiralling upwards as he did so. I watched how he did it. I needed to relax.

But Samuel would not let the matter rest. He did not realize that I now believed in his dream more than he did. In order, as he thought, to convince me, he told me a story.

He was still a baby in arms, he said, when some kind of epidemic struck the little village on the bank of the Bodrog river. Babies were the first to suffer. They refused to suck their mothers' milk, clamping their lips tight shut whenever they were offered the breast.

Little Samuel became seriously ill. He was not the Friedmanns' only child, but he was the youngest and the one they loved the most. Papa and Mama Friedmann always loved their latest-born the best.

Doctor after doctor came and examined the child, looked at his tongue, peered at his throat, tapped his chest, prescribed medicines they said would certainly cure him, collected their fat fees and left. And Samuel grew steadily worse.

Grandma was in despair. She put cold compresses on the child and murmured healing sayings over him. Then she lit candles and prayed. She prayed with tears and, when no more tears would come, she prayed dry-eyed. Her prayers were answered; she had a dream! Sitting in a chair by her mortally ill grandson, she had a dream.

She fell asleep and dreamt that a voice, a friendly yet exhortatory voice, spoke to her. 'Listen to me,' the voice told her. 'I am sending you a professor, a great professor. Tell him to cure your child. He will cure him.'

Grandma woke up. The candles were still burning; the cocks were already crowing; the young calf in the byre lowed once; the dog barked twice; then everything was quiet. Grandma looked at the child. He was still breathing—slowly and with difficulty, but breathing. She looked to the left and to the right. There was nobody else in the room. She opened the window. There was nobody to be seen. The only sign of movement was the flickering flame of a small oil-lamp at the mast-head of a ship on the river. A black and white cat ran noiselessly along the street. In a neighbouring birch, a bird was singing: Cheep, cheep, cheep.

Only a sliver of moon could be seen. Grandma closed the window softly and whispered: 'It was one of God's angels.' She raised both arms and threw back her head, her eyes on the ceiling. 'Oh God, please fulfil my dream, oh God, oh God.' Her lips did not move, for she was praying in her heart. She looked like a saint, and perhaps she was one. She looked carefully at the little creature asleep in his cot. His little chest was still rising and falling. She blew out the candles. Day had broken.

Mr Friedmann was already up and dressed. He tiptoed into the room and looked anxiously at the child. 'He's still breathing.' The worst, the thing he had feared most of all, had not happened yet. Grandma whispered: 'A professor, a professor.'

'What? What did you say?'

'Yes, yes, a professor will come.' Mr Friedmann did not know what she was talking about. 'What do you mean, a professor will come?'

'Just what I said. I dreamt it, a heavenly angel told me.' Mr Friedmann did not know what to say, so he remained silent and merely shrugged his shoulders.

The church bells were ringing, as they did every day at noon. Grandma took a bucket and went to the well to fetch some water. What a deep well it was. A carriage was standing by it, while the coachman watered his two horses. It was no ordinary carriage, it was a princely, even a regal carriage. Nor did the coachman look like most of his fellows. No ordinary coachman wore a spotless livery like that, with gleaming buttons of gold. At least, they looked like gold. They were certainly gilded. And one did not see white horses like those every day.

A crowd of barefoot children stood staring at the unusual sight. Grandma went and stood behind them and subjected the passenger in the carriage to a critical examination as he sat there on the comfortably upholstered rear seat. He did not have any gold buttons, and he was completely bald, except for a few grey hairs. A leather bag lay on the seat beside him. Grandma thought that it could be a doctor's bag. One could imagine such an honourable man being a doctor and a royal highness as well.

Grandma was a shrewd judge. The coachman proudly confirmed that the gentleman was indeed a doctor, a famous doctor, a professor. And the coach was a princely one. It belonged to the high-born count, whose wife lay mortally ill.

As soon as Grandma heard the word 'professor', she did not want to hear any more, and lost interest in the rest of the loquacious coachman's account. Now she knew for certain that one of God's angels had taken a hand in matters. A royal coach, a gold-braided coachman, a famous professor, all together —this was heaven's doing. She wanted to fall on her knees, but Jewish women do not kneel, any more than Jewish men do, except once a year, in synagogue. That is how their religion ordains it. So she half-knelt. 'Professor, professor,' she entreated, 'my little grandson is in danger. I beg of you, please come and see him. There,' she pointed to the house, 'there he lies, my little, sick grandchild.'

The professor needed no second bidding. Although he looked a little surprised, he took his leather bag and hurried after Grandma. 'Please excuse the mess,' she said as they entered the house,

31

but the professor did not pay any attention to the mess.

He did not want to see the baby's tongue, nor did he look at his throat or tap his chest. One look at the tiny patient was enough for the professor. He opened his bag, took out a small bottle, shook it, and gave it to Grandma. 'Five drops every hour, night and day for three days,' he told her, and turned to go. Papa Friedmann stood there, with a thick wallet in his hand.

'How much for your trouble, Professor?' he asked.

'Nothing.' Mr Friedmann stared at him. Incredible. Grandma, too, stared—Mrs Friedmann was no less amazed.

'Last night,' the professor related, 'an awesome voice spoke to me and said: "A woman will ask you to heal her grandchild, I command you to do so!" If heaven commands it, then heaven will pay the bill with spiritual means. I will accept no earthly payment.' Then he left. Mr and Mrs Friedmann stood as if thunderstruck. Once more Grandma raised her hands and eyes to heaven, and she, too, stood there silently for a considerable time.

INTO THE GESTAPO NET

Our train journey finally ended at Rakamaz, the enchantingly beautiful country village one and a half miles to the south of my home village of Tokay. 'Everybody out. This is as far as the train goes.' The Germans had blocked the strategically important Theis Bridge between Tokay and Rakamaz.

Our attempt to reach home via the road bridge came to grief—'Use of this bridge by Jews prohibited,' a notice said. Samuel could not keep back his tears. 'What will become of us now?' he wailed. Personally I saw no reason for concern. After all, I had a very good friend there, Ferenc, a business friend of my father's. What a wonderful man, and how he loved children. He was a remarkable person, a real gentleman! Whenever he was invited to a business conference at our house he never once failed to lavish endearments on us children. There was no doubt whatever that he would help and advise us.

A large garden filled with a colourful mass of flowers led to his magnificent green-and-yellow painted luxury villa. The iron garden gate was unbolted, and although an Alsatian sitting under a pear-tree observed us closely as we walked in, he did not molest us. He just sat there contentedly, wagging his tail.

So great was my joy at being about to see my 'great friend' again, that I almost forgot that times had changed when the Germans had marched in. I hurried up to the door and, heedless of the babel of voices that assailed my ears from within, raised my right hand to the catch. But before I had touched it, Samuel pulled me back with such force that I nearly fell over. 'Come away, come away!' he whispered excitedly. He wasted no time on further explanations, but raced out from the garden at top speed like a hunted animal. From the street he beckoned to me despairingly to follow him, but I paid no attention, wondering to myself in a confused manner whether he had gone out of his mind. Then I became aware of the loud voices inside the villa. There must have been a great many people there, singing, making merry and clapping. A birthday party perhaps, or even Ferenc celebrating his wedding. That would be a fine time to come bursting in. I put my ear to the door to try and find out what sort of celebration was going on, and could hardly believe what I heard. Suddenly I realized clearly what had caused Samuel to run away. Could this really be happening? Were they really toasting Szalasi and Hitler, wishing them strength and long life?

However, I quickly recovered from my momentary confusion and decided to make sure that I had heard aright. I leapt forward, turned the handle and opened the door. As soon as I had done so, I wanted to turn and run, but it was too late. The singing tailed off and the beer-drinking company turned their eyes on me. The expression on their faces was unmistakable: 'What does the fellow want?' Ferenc was one of the first to see me. He was unpleasantly surprised and his face grew red. For a moment he did not know how to react. His eyes opened wide, and he looked shiftily round the room. Then he pushed himself to his feet and kicked his bright blue chair aside, giving it such a powerful shove with the toe of his heavy winter boot that it clattered against the stove. Before I realized what was happening, he had poured the contents of a water pitcher over me. As I turned and ran I heard uproar from the room behind me. Something hard smashed into my leg, thrown by someone in the villa, but the pain, great though it was, hurt less than the spiritual blow I had received. 'I warned you,' was all Samuel had to say.

We sat down in the shadow of a wall and stayed there on the ground for a while, silent and not knowing what to do next. My head dropped forward and I began to doze off. Suddenly, Samuel leapt to his feet as a torrent of muddy, evil-smelling water cascaded down on us. I could hardly trust my own eyes when I looked up and saw that the person who had poured the water over us was none other than Ferenc's nephew, Pista, who was the same age as myself and whom his uncle had often brought with him when he visited our house. I had always been so friendly towards him, lent him my bicycle so that he could learn to ride, given him all my toys to play with—and now, this. Times had indeed changed.

'Is this all that's left of our friendship?' I asked him. In reply, he stuck out his tongue and raised the bucket threateningly. Samuel was wise to take me by the arm and drag me hurriedly away.

'This is not the time for a fight,' he said.

I was utterly exhausted. My innate propensity for believing in people had been swamped by a veritable ocean of disillusionment. Carrying our luggage, we wandered aimlessly about the village, waiting for some kind of miracle to happen. We were overjoyed when I spotted Mr Rosenbaum slipping out of a narrow side street. Before venturing into the main road, he glanced anxiously to right and left as if he were frightened of something. He lived in the village and we knew each other slightly. He was very helpful. He took us home with him and advised us to try and reach Bodrog-Keresztur by a roundabout route. There was one obstacle, of course, the Bodrog River, which we would have to cross on our way. However, Mr Rosenbaum was sure that we would have no difficulty in crossing by the ferry. We took his advice and set out. There was no road, and we had to make our own way across fields and through woods. Every time we heard a noise we stopped and dropped to the ground. Only later did we learn what a dangerous route we had followed. Apparently a group of political prisoners had overpowered their guards and escaped when the Germans marched in, and the Germans were looking for them. Any who were caught were shot on the spot. As a matter of fact, several totally innocent forestry workers who were unlucky enough to cross the Germans' path were also taken away and shot out of hand.

Samuel's spirits rose as his home came in sight, especially when we could see the actual house he lived in. There was the very long, straggling village, sprawling along the opposite bank of the river. The bank we were standing on was totally uninhabited. It was just a meadow. The snow had begun to melt, but there were still some four hard-packed inches of it covering the ground.

We were not far from the ferry point when we met the first person we had seen on our trek from

Ferenc's villa, a shepherd. 'Where are you going, children?' he asked in surprise.

'Home,' replied Samuel. 'Have you got passes? Nobody is allowed to cross without a pass,' said the shepherd. 'German soldiers are on guard at the ferry, and Jews are not given a pass. I'm warning you now, don't show yourselves near the ferry!'

Water was scarce in the village, since there was no piped supply and the wells were not particularly bountiful. The women used the river to do their laundry. Neither Samuel nor I regarded it as a coincidence that his thirteen-year-old sister should be doing some washing on the river bank. We both considered it an act of Providence. When they saw each other, they burst into tears. We hardly noticed the yellow star on her breast. It must be the latest fashion, if not from Paris, then from Berlin. 'Wait there, I'm going to tell Daddy,' she shouted and ran off.

My eyes were riveted on the little hills. How secretive, how mysterious they now seemed to me. There the great rabbi lay at rest, the great rabbi whose prophecies my teacher had told me about only yesterday. I could not get Samuel's dream out of my head, and felt that something extraordinary was soon to befall me.

My thoughts and glances were still on the hills

with the sun setting behind them when Samuel's sister came back and shouted to us to go to the ferry as 'everything has been taken care of'. We did not merely walk to the ferry, we ran as fast as we could. It was ready to cast off to take us to the other side of the river. Our knees knocked together when we saw two sentries on the opposite bank pointing the muzzles of their machine-guns at us. A third man stood behind them, his legs spread wide. He was dressed in a magnificent uniform and held a pair of binoculars to his eyes. 'Danger! Danger!' the Hungarian ferryman whispered to us before we climbed aboard. 'The Germans are extremely brutal and merciless,' he added softly as the ferry began to move forward.

'Oh God, please do not let Samuel's dream be fulfilled,' I prayed, although I could not suppress my tears. Samuel was white-faced, his eyes shut tight. He did not want to see the murderous shooting begin. But nothing happened—not yet.

We had hardly set foot on dry land, when the elegantly uniformed officer with the snow-white gloves barred our path. He looked us over searchingly from head to foot. Seething with animal rage, he unloosed a stream of curses and threats at us and at a certain notary as yet unknown to us.

'These are children? These are Jews! That damned

notary deceived me. I'll teach that damned Jewish lackey a good lesson. I'll teach him that Jews aren't children. They are Bolsheviks, white slave traders and such things. It is unparalleled impudence to cause me, a German officer, to be put to all this trouble over a couple of Jews.'

Mr Friedmann had asked the notary public, with whom he was friendly, to help him and see that we were allowed to cross the river. He had telephoned the German commandant of the village for permission for two children waiting across the river to be allowed to use the ferry. The commandant agreed, but stipulated that he wanted to see them himself. The notary, with commendable foresight, had omitted to say to what race the children belonged.

We were escorted to the village assembly hall. There, the German commandant and the notary almost came to blows over the complicated legal question as to whether young Jews could be called children or not. The notary took the position that there was no ruling on the subject in the Hungarian code of law. He refused to accept the commandant's assertions that German law had replaced Hungarian law since the day before.

When the clamour had died down a little we were asked for our identity papers. The notary testified that he knew Samuel personally and that he lived in the village. Samuel was told that he could go. He heaved a sigh of relief, pressed my hand quickly and disappeared at speed.

'And who is this then?' The notary looked at my identity papers. 'He lives in the next village, Tokay,' he said. The officer turned to me. 'And what business have you here?' he demanded.

'The Theis Bridge was blocked, so I couldn't reach home that way. I was trying to get there by way of this village,' I replied.

'What is your profession?'

'I am a student.'

'Aha, studying Marxism-Leninism.'

'No, that is incorrect.'

'What then?'

'Mathematics.'

'Aha, so you want to become a banker!'

'No, I never wanted to become a banker.'

'You can tell that to the Marines. You are all bankers.'

'Hold him here,' the officer ordered the notary. 'I'll think over what to do with him.' He marched out of the room.

'Don't worry, son,' the notary told me. 'You will soon be home with your parents.'

'I hope God will make that come true, but I'm afraid——'

41

'Afraid of what?'

'I have evil forebodings.'

'Evil forebodings? I can imagine that you are afraid of the Germans. They are a bestial rabble. But their end is so near now. The Russians are on the border and it's only a matter of a few weeks, or perhaps even days.'

'I don't know myself what I am afraid of. You know, Mr Notary, yesterday and today have seemed so mysterious to me. Unfathomable dreams, strange meetings——'

'Oh stop talking about your dreams. If I were to think about the dreams I have had, I would not enjoy one peaceful day. The nonsense I have dreamed in my life. Hold your head high! Keep your spirits up!'

A man in the next room, he must have been a local council employee, brought in a bottle of golden Tokay. 'I'll show you how to raise your spirits,' he exclaimed, throwing back his head and emptying half the bottle down his throat. Then he passed the bottle to the notary, who needed no second bidding. However, he did not empty the bottle completely. He left some wine in it for me. 'You are so young,' he said, holding out the bottle. But I refused. At home in Tokay I had not been taught to drown my cares in the local wine.

The telephone rang.

'Assembly hall here. Who's that speaking?'

'Mr Samet, President of the Jewish community,' said a voice from the other end of the wire.

'Good evening Mr Samet, can I help you?'

'I have just heard that a young relative of mine, a boy, has been arrested by the Germans.'

'Arrested—that's rather too strong an expression. As a matter of fact he is sitting here near me in a well-heated room.'

'What do they want with a sixteen-year-old boy? He hasn't committed any crime.'

'Oh, my dear Mr Samet, since yesterday everything has been in utter confusion. But I am looking after the boy all right and we will make sure that he gets home safely to his parents.'

'Thank you very much, Mr Notary. I am sure you will do everything you can for him, but since it will soon be the Sabbath, I would very much like to take him to my home until Sunday.'

'Agreed. However, it will be difficult to arrange unless you come to the assembly hall yourself to collect him and sign a declaration that the boy is a minor. It is only a formality.'

'Good, thank you. I'll be there shortly.'

'Good-bye, Mr Samet.'

'Good-bye.'

'Now, my boy, you will be able to spend the Sabbath with your relatives. Are you pleased?'

'Very, Mr Notary. Thank you.'

At that moment someone dashed hastily into the room. He was so out of breath that he could not speak, but when he had recovered to some extent, he burst out: 'What has happened?' He stopped and took several deep breaths before continuing. 'I have just come from headquarters. That German is cursing about you, in a shocking manner. He is talking about killing, about shooting. What is it all about?'

'Shooting? Who is going to be shot?' the notary asked agitatedly.

'I don't know. I could only understand half of what he was saying, but I kept on hearing the word "Jew! Jew!" and I heard him order his telephone operator to obtain a permit to shoot somebody.'

The notary waved the messenger away and came towards me visibly perturbed. He took my arm fondly and led me into the next room. 'I'll be back soon, my son,' he said, as he went out and closed the door behind him. But he did not notice that he had not closed it properly. Through the crack I could hear every word that was being spoken in the next room.

'I understand everything that is going on. The boy is in danger, deadly danger. The Germans are hunting for the political prisoners who have broken out of captivity and have given orders that anyone suspicious found wandering about the fields and woods is to be shot.

'His hatred of Jews knows no bounds. If he had realized before that a Jewish boy was involved he would have had him shot on the pretext of being a suspect. I have managed to avert the worst and get the boy out of his clutches. That's why he's in such a rage. Apparently he is seeking some further pretext to do him some harm. We have to prevent it!'

'But how?' exclaimed the other man.

'We'll try and get the police to help.'

I heard the receiver being picked up. 'This is the assembly hall here, the public notary speaking. Send us two policemen at once, we are having trouble with the Germans. You must intervene. A young boy is in danger. Come at once, before it's too late.'

There was a pause, and then the notary exclaimed: 'What's going on? Haven't we got an independent country any more? Haven't we got a government, police? This is disgraceful!' He banged down the receiver.

'It's incredible. They have strict orders to remain in barracks and not interfere in German concerns. If only Mr Samet would get here soon, that would be the best solution just now.'

The door opened and the notary was soon standing next to me, stroking my face and saying, 'Everything will be all right,' but he did not sound very convinced of it himself. Then he looked impatiently at his watch and muttered, 'Oh, Mr Samet . . .'

Only a few seconds later, somebody knocked on the door of the next room. For a moment the notary shook with fright, but then he pulled himself together and thought. No, it was not the Gestapo. They were not in the habit of knocking. It must be Mr Samet. And so it was.

'Ah, dear Mr Samet. You have come just at the right moment. Take the boy and bring him back tomorrow evening. Then we will make sure he gets to his parents. And you, son,' he turned to me and patted my shoulder, 'stay indoors all day and do not show yourself on the street.' He took Mr Samet aside and whispered something in his ear.

When we reached the street, Mr Samet exclaimed to me: 'Now you are free!'

I was no stranger to Mr Samet's house, for I had often been there on visits with my father and grandfather. It was about 300 yards from the assembly hall. We walked past the house where the dead wonder rabbi used to live. Although I knew that I ought to hurry and get off the street as quickly as possible, I could not resist stopping in front of the

46

rabbi's house. It drew me like a magnet. With my forehead pressed to the wall, I stood and prayed, and this was probably the first time in my life that my tears had flowed so readily. But Mr Samet was urging me to come on, so I reluctantly dragged myself away from the famous house.

We were perhaps ten paces or less from where the Samet family lived, when we heard a squealing of brakes so close behind us that the grey-haired Mr Samet jumped aside like a young boy. Before the vehicle had stopped completely, there was a loud blast on the horn. 'Jew, back to the assembly hall!' yelled the raucous voice of that same Gestapo man who had dealt with me before. 'And you,' he shouted at Mr Samet, 'make yourself scarce, or else . . .' I had no choice but to obey the shouted order.

ON THE WAY TO
EXECUTION

Once inside the assembly hall, the S.S. man kicked the door closed with his gleaming jackboot. Before the notary, who had an idea that something was amiss, could hasten in from the next room, the Gestapo man started cursing in Prussian dialect, pouring out a stream of foul language, much of it incomprehensible.

'Who gave you permission to let the boy go?' he thundered at the notary at the top of his voice, saliva dribbling down his chin. Drawing his pistol, he put it to the notary's chest. The notary reacted bravely. Without a sign of fear and with no hint of deference in his voice he said: 'The law imposes on me the duty of taking care of minors when parental influence is lacking for any reason whatsoever or when, as in this case, it can temporarily not be exercised. This duty I fulfilled, and I do not like being vulgarly abused for doing so.'

'Ha . . . The law! He comes to me with laws made by the Jews and Jewish lackeys. He doesn't know yet that a new epoch dawned yesterday. But he soon will know about it! As for the Jew, now I'll take him in hand myself. I'll relieve you of your duty,' he concluded sarcastically.

Then he turned to me. 'Come with me,' he commanded, and marched quickly out of the room. I stayed where I was for a moment. 'Please, please,' I besought the notary, 'don't let him take me away. He'll kill me, I can feel it.'

'My dear child,' replied the notary, 'you can see for yourself what sort of people we are up against. I am powerless to help you . . .'

The Gestapo man rushed back into the room, brandishing his pistol. 'You filthy dog, do you think you can keep a German officer waiting? Get moving, or else I'll finish you both off!'

Soon I realized that we were on our way back to the ferry. Once again we passed the wonder rabbi's house, but this time I could not stop. My eyes were turned to the house, but tears dimmed my sight. People stared curiously from their windows, silent and unsmiling. Some of them waved to me. An old woman cursed and waved her walking stick at us, muttering something as we went past. I could not make out whether her curses were meant for me or my escort.

Two German soldiers came towards us. After a resounding Hitler salute, one of them asked: 'Where are you going with the boy, then?'

'I'm going to take him across the river on the ferry and then kill him.'

'How can you? You know we are forbidden to shoot.'

'Oh that's quite easy. He'll be shot while trying to escape!'

'Well, that's different. If you do it that way, it's all right, of course. Heil Hitler.'

Now there was no longer any doubt about my impending fate. The last lesson our teacher had given us went through my mind: 'Man has the duty to give thanks to Heaven for everything that happens to him, good or bad.' Inner peace and joy came over me, and my fear vanished. How unhappy people without faith must be, when faced with a fate like mine. How comfortless the thought must be that one was about to be totally destroyed. On the other hand, how full of happiness was the knowledge that one's soul could never be put to death, never wiped out by the flames of destruction. That it would emerge unscathed from the murderous salvoes that would annihilate one's body.

So immersed had I been in my thoughts, that I had not noticed that we had reached the ferry. Hundreds of curious people had gathered there, all of them looking at me. I paid them no attention, however. I did not want to squander the last few minutes still vouchsafed to me, but to use them for inner reflection. 'How mysterious the world is,' I thought to myself, 'how unfathomable the course of events. The lamb is devoured by the wolf, the dog hunts the cat, the cat hunts the mouse, and the fish opens and closes its mouth the whole time. And what of human beings? Things are no different with them; the strong devour the weak. What irony it is that man imagines himself to be the highest form of life on earth!'

I was jolted out of my thoughts by a sudden uproar. The ferryman had refused to take me across. I was not certain, but I had the impression that he knew, or at least guessed, what was to happen and did not wish to have any part in it. Even when the Gestapo man threatened to shoot him, he refused point-blank to ferry me across the river. Threats to shoot people fell thick and fast at that particular period of time.

Someone in the crowd said that he knew how to operate the ferry. 'All right, get in,' I was ordered. I did so. The Gestapo man stayed on the village side of the river with the two German soldiers.

As the ferry began to move, I offered all the money I had with me to the ferryman, begging him: 'Please go slowly.' The ferryman granted my plea. I wanted to buy time for one last prayer.

The hill-top cemetery where the wonder rabbi's grave was, was clearly visible from the ferry. I could even see the little stone structure erected over the grave in his honour. Thousands of pilgrims used to visit it to pray there. It drew my glances irresistibly. It seemed as if the wonder rabbi's prophecy that all the suffering would start with me was about to come true. Would his promise also come true, that he would stand by me and ease my pain?

Just before the ferry reached the shore I noticed that the Gestapo man was taking aim at me with his carbine. As soon as the ferry touched land I leapt out like a flash, bent myself double and ran, zig-zagging as I went. Bang! A shot rang out and something hit my body with a tremendous shock. I fell to the ground.

THE DREAM

I felt that the wound must be somewhere below my shoulder, because that was where the blood was coming from. I tried to stop the flow by pressing my right arm against my ribs, but in vain. A crowd had gathered on the opposite bank of the river and were excitedly discussing what had happened. 'He is still alive, he is still alive!' some of them shouted, while others cried, 'No, no, he is already dead!' But the Gestapo man knew exactly what the situation was. Standing with his feet apart, he put his binoculars to his eyes and focused them on me, calling out scornfully: 'Kri, kri, kri.' I felt myself growing steadily weaker, and then everything went black and I lost consciousness.

When I came to, night had fallen and some minutes elapsed before I could remember what had happened. There was not so much as a glimmer of light visible anywhere, just thick blackness. A damp, clinging mist hid the stars from view, and I shivered with cold. 'I must get up and try to get some help somewhere,' I thought to myself. 'On the other side of the river there is a whole village full of people who would certainly help me, but there is no way of getting across.' Finally, I decided to go back to Rakamaz, 15 miles or so away, to Mr Rosenbaum, who had taken me in before, with no questions asked. Just as I was scrambling to my feet, a flare burst overhead and lit up all the surroundings. I flattened myself on the ground again, and then lost consciousness once more. It must have been long past midnight when I came to. The mist had lifted and the sky was powdered with stars. The snow, which had started to melt during the day, had frozen hard again. I tried to get up, but my coat had frozen to the ground and I could not free it. I wriggled and squirmed like an eel until, finally, I managed to tear myself away from the ground and stand up on unsteady feet. My legs felt swollen and heavy, a sign, though I did not know it, that they were frozen. At my first attempt to take a step forward I fell down and hit my head hard on the ice. My hands were frozen too and I was unable to use them to help break my fall. But I persisted in my attempts to walk and fell down a second time, again hitting my head on the ice. This happened ten, fifteen, twenty times, until I no longer had the strength to get up. I felt something warm trickling down my forehead and neck. It was blood from my head and nose. The gunshot wound seemed to have stopped bleeding, but every time I coughed I brought

54

up blood from my injured lung. Pushing myself along on my back I reached an oak tree whose thick trunk served as a support for my head. The night seemed to last an eternity, and then, as the first streaks of dawn appeared on the horizon, I fell into a deep sleep. When I awoke, the snow was melting again for, according to the calendar, spring had arrived, and in the spring the sun shines. The date was March 21, 1944.

Now I could have a look at myself. My hands, feet, head, nose and chest were exactly as Samuel had seen them in his dream: 'I saw you lying on the ground, covered with blood and in a dreadful state.' And the wonder rabbi's prophecy to my grandfather had come true: 'Your grandson will be the first to suffer in this country.' Would the rest of what he had said also come true? 'I will stand by him to ease his suffering.' My glance turned to the other side of the river, to where the village lay bathed in sunshine. There was not a sign of movement. It was as if the whole village had died. Then came the sound of a drum. Everyone would know that it heralded an important announcement, for here the drummer took the place of the radio, newspapers and posters. He was the official announcer for the authorities. All I could hear was the sound of the drum. I was too far away to hear what was being announced. Later, others told me what it had been: 'Attention, attention, here is an urgent announcement. The German command warns everybody to keep away from the wounded spy and not to try and help him. Anyone disobeying this order will be shot!' A white pigeon perched on a branch above my head. It too seemed to have little to be happy about. Who knew, I thought to myself, whether this pigeon was not thinking: 'Oh God, why am I hunted and tormented by everyone? Why do all the big birds want to kill me? I have not done anybody any harm.'

A raging thirst gripped me and I turned over onto my stomach and began to suck up some of the melting snow. So thirsty was I that I did not care about the earth mixed with it. As the sun set, an icy wind began to blow, and it whistled angrily through the bare branches of the oak tree. Then, when I had recited the evening prayer, I felt such enormous spiritual power come over me, as I had never felt in my life before. This was a message from heaven. I could hear a voice telling me not to be afraid, for God was with me and would save me. Filled with hope and an inexplicable happiness, I let the howling wind lull me into a deep sleep.

When I awoke again, I heard something moving about near me and opened my eyes fearfully to see who or what it was. I saw a big, black dog, which came peacefully towards me and licked the dried blood off my clothes. Then it began to lick my blood-smeared face. Afterwards the dog lay down beside me and I fell asleep again.

As I slept, I had a dream. I saw a gigantic pillar of fire reaching to the sky, and it lit up the surroundings so powerfully, that I could not bear to look at it.

A fierce west wind howled all around, moving houses from their foundations and uprooting trees. The wind fanned the flames of the pillar of fire, and blew them in all directions, so that the whole world seemed to be engulfed in a sea of roaring flames. Slowly, the unbearably bright light began to grow dimmer and then disappeared altogether as everything became blotted out by clouds of thick, black smoke. In the middle of it I could discern the shining figure of a man clothed from head to foot in a flowing, snow-white garment. He had large blue eyes and a silvery-grey beard down to his waist, and his eyes glowed with light, sending out beams of it in all the colours of the spectrum. I looked at him in wonder, unable to divert my gaze from those luminous eyes. He stood there silently, without moving and looked at me.

'Who are you?' I asked anxiously.

He continued to stand there, silent and unmoving, and again I asked him: 'Who are you? Tell me who you are.'

Slowly he seated himself next to me on the ground, took my right hand lovingly in his and said softly: 'I am the person for whom you wanted to light candles.'

I reached for the candles in my pocket to give them to him, but he gently declined: 'No my child, it is no longer necessary to light candles,' he said. 'I have lit a candle for you instead. It burns with an eternal flame and will never be extinguished.'

'What will happen to me?'

'That is what I have come to tell you.'

'Are you going to take me with you?'

'Oh no, for I am no longer on earth. I live in a totally different world.'

'Is it beautiful there?'

'Very beautiful.'

'Please take me there.'

'I cannot.'

'Why?'

'Because your time has not yet come.'

'Then why have you come to me?'

'To ease your suffering.'

'I feel so wretched and alone here.'

'Do not worry my child. You will soon be taken away from here.'

'Where to?'

'Somewhere where you will be healed.'

'Is that certain?'

'If I tell you so, yes.'

'And then I won't have to suffer any more?'

'You will still have to suffer a great deal, but you will survive if you do not lose your faith.'

'Why must I suffer so much?'

'A believer does not ask such questions.'

'Will you stay with me now?'

'That I cannot do.'

'Why am I so alone here?'

'One is never alone. The Almighty is everywhere.'

'My teacher, your son-in-law, charged me with the task of asking you to pray for him.'

'I always pray for him and for everyone.'

'Tell me, please, how long must I continue to suffer?'

'I am not allowed to tell you.'

'Why?'

'I have no permission to do so.'

'Who gives you your orders?'

'He who gives orders to the sun, the moon and the stars.'

He pressed my hand in parting and rose to go. I held him fast. 'One more question. Who will take me away from here?'

'The devil.'

'The devil?' I gasped.

'Do not be amazed. When heaven desires it, the devil is also benevolent.'

The black smoke dissolved and the shining figure disappeared. I woke up, bathed in sweat, and saw that the dog was still lying near me. He was looking at me watchfully, moving his ears now and again.

I fell asleep yet again, and when I awoke daylight had come. I turned my glance towards the site of the wonder rabbi's tomb, for it was he who had appeared to me in my dream. As I lay there, I looked all round me to see if the devil the wonder rabbi had spoken of was coming. I was curious to see what he looked like, although I was worried that I might faint with fright when I saw him.

THE PRIEST
AND THE RESCUE

Atop the bare hill, lonely and apparently deserted, the high tower of the ornate mediaeval church reared towards the crystal-clear sky. The golden coloured bells, sparkling in the rays of the sun, hung motionless and silent in the belfry. A young priest, inducted only a few days earlier, paced up and down across the stone-paved churchyard, debating with himself what to do. Every so often he ran over to the tower, climbed quickly to the top, poked his head out of the narrow opening and watched something through field glasses. 'He is alive, he is still alive,' he murmured to himself, as he climbed back down the steep steps, his face grave. He hastened from one saintly effigy to the next, falling to his knees before each one, hoping that they would speak to him and give him guidance in this difficult hour of decision, telling him how to act and what to do. Should he remain enclosed within the four walls of his church and wait in silence while, outside, a man died? Could this be reconciled with Christian teaching? On the other hand, could he imperil many lives in order perhaps to save one? Then he thought he heard a voice which told him to act. Once more he climbed the tower and began to tug at the bell-rope. It was midday. The plates of hot soup already stood steaming on snow-white table-cloths in every home in the village. The newly inducted priest must have a very important announcement to make if he was calling his flock to church at this unusual hour, his parishioners thought to themselves as they hurried out of their houses. They did not know for sure what it was all about, but they had some kind of idea that it could only concern the boy lying across the river in a pool of his own blood, since he had been the sole topic of conversation in the village all day.

The church had never been so crowded before. Even the grey-haired village blacksmith was there, a man who, in the ordinary way, was by no means convinced of the holiness of the Madonna. As the priest mounted the pulpit with confident tread, his congregation waited tensely to hear what he had to say.

The priest's voice was noticeably agitated as he began: 'Today, within sight of our village, an innocent boy was dreadfully maltreated. All of you know this. For two days now he has been lying in a pool of his own blood. We have seen him with our own eyes, but we have not raised a finger to help him. It is true that they threatened to shoot us if we approached him, but is that any justification for our inactivity? Shall we be able to excuse ourselves before God when he demands a reckoning from us? Of course not! However, it is still not too late for us to rectify our shortcomings, for we can all see that he is still alive. Are we to continue doing nothing until the boy dies in misery and suffering before our very eyes? Or shall we do something to help him, and do it all together?'

Everyone replied: 'We will help him, we are prepared to help him. We will go at once to the German headquarters and force them to help. There is not a minute to be lost. We must abandon our midday meals, or else it may be too late.'

The bells rang out again, and the entire village, young and old alike, converged on the German headquarters. I heard the sound of shouting: 'Murderers! Barbarians! Sadists!' It continued for an hour, or perhaps two, and then everything grew strangely still. The sun was setting, and soon only half of it was visible above the horizon, like half an apple someone had cut off with a knife. Then it disappeared completely from the rose-coloured sky.

The dog was still lying quietly beside me on the ground, but it suddenly became uneasy and began to bark loudly. Then heavy footsteps sounded from behind me. I looked up and saw two tall S.S. men coming towards me. When I saw that they were carrying spades I broke out in a cold sweat. One said: 'He's still alive,' and raised his pistol. Slipping off the safety catch, he aimed at my head. Like a flash, his companion knocked the gun out of his hand and it went off as it hit the ground. A bullet ripped into the earth nearby.

'Do you think I want to waste my free Sunday digging a grave in this iron-hard ground? It would be much more fun to go dancing with our girl friends.'

'You're right, mate, but what shall we do with him?'

'Oh, that's no problem. We'll take him to the hospital and that's the end of the matter as far as we're concerned.'

They turned on their heels and began to walk off, calling the dog to follow them: 'Fafi, Fafi, come on Fafi.' The dog got up and followed them and I heard one of them say: 'Fafi didn't do his job this time. Instead of tearing him to pieces, he just lay down beside him.'

About a quarter of an hour later, they came back in a car, threw me into the back and took me to the ferry. When we reached the other side the whole village was waiting for us, the priest in their midst.

They waved to me and pressed forward to shake my hand, but the S.S. men pushed them back. They threw me chocolate and sweets but none of it landed anywhere near me.

The car took me to Sarospatak and stopped in front of the hospital. One of the S.S. men went inside and came back with a stretcher. They put me on it and carried me inside. When the nurse came along to admit me, one of the S.S. men said: 'We found the boy lying in a field. He seems to have been hit by a stray bullet.' Then they walked out.

But it was a military hospital and I could not stay there, so an ambulance took me to the temporary Jewish hospital in Satoraljaujhely. Actually, there had been a Jewish hospital in the town for very many years, but the building had been taken over by the Hungarian army, so a temporary hospital had been set up in a school. The assistant doctor, Dr Blau, took one look at me and made a despairing gesture, as if to say: 'There's no hope for this one.' The first thing I asked the nurse for was a hot bath. 'If I let you have a bath I'd be a murderess,' she replied.

The next day, I had my first visitor, a Gestapo man. 'How are you getting on?' he asked in a friendly manner.

'You don't have to ask. You can see for yourself,' I answered.

'What happened to you, then?'

'Since you have come here to see me, you must know.'

'I was told that you had been hit by a stray bullet.'

'Not a word of truth in it.'

'Well who did shoot you, then?'

'The S.S.'

The friendliness vanished from his face abruptly.

'Impossible. That would be unthinkable. My investigations show that you were hit by a stray bullet. I advise you not to make these false accusations, because we shall not submit to being slandered.'

He wished me better and went out, after leaving a bar of chocolate on my night table.

Later on, the nurse came in with a thermometer. She noticed the chocolate and remarked: 'Oh what a nice present you have got.' She tore open the wrapper, broke off a piece of chocolate and wanted to put it in my mouth. In the next bed to me was a Viennese who had been forced to flee from Austria, been interned and was now in hospital because he had fallen ill. The moment he saw the nurse trying to put a piece of the Gestapo man's chocolate in my mouth, he leapt out of bed and snatched it out of her hand. The nurse stared at him in speechless amazement. 'Don't you think, nurse, that that chocolate might be poisoned?' he said to her.

'Don't talk nonsense. It's Szerencs' chocolate, made in Hungary.'

'That I don't deny, but it could still be poisoned. We can soon find out.'

'How?'

There were a number of stray dogs in the hospital grounds, and my ward-mate opened the window and threw one of them the piece of chocolate the nurse had just wanted to give me. The dog gulped it down and a few minutes later lay dead on the ground. Many of the patients were standing at the window and saw what happened. The nurse burst into tears. 'If this gentleman had not snatched the chocolate out of my hand, I would have killed the boy,' she sobbed.

That same evening there was a telephone call from the Gestapo enquiring about my health. The hospital office had been informed of what had happened, so they told the Gestapo that my case was hopeless. The Gestapo did not make any more enquiries.

Although Jews were forbidden to travel, my mother came to visit me. She said that, on Saturday, while I was still lying in the field, a Hungarian

67

peasant had come to our house, claiming to have visited me in the field and to have brought me food and something to drink. He demanded a suitable sum of money for his services. This item of information amazed me and I had to tell my mother that there was not a word of truth in it.

I would have to have an operation, but it was not easy to find a doctor to agree to perform it, since the word had gone round that the Gestapo had forbidden it. Finally, they brought in a doctor from outside who had not heard of the ban, and he performed the operation. The bullet wound healed eventually, but I could not use my hands or feet for a long time afterwards because they had been frozen.

From Bodrog-Keresztur, the priest sent a messenger to tell me that the whole village wished me well. This man declared that all the villagers were saying that I would surely survive the war, after such a great miracle had happened to me. He showed me a press cutting which said: 'The Jewish boy, J. Schwarz, who lived in Tokay, had been shot by the Germans while trying to escape. There was a strong suspicion that he was a Communist spy. His condition was serious.'

YOUNG GABOR

The situation of the Jews grew daily worse. Ghettoes were set up in the capital of every province and all the Jews shut up there. My parents, together with all the other Jews in my home village, were sent to Satoraljaujhely where I was in hospital, and it was in these unhappy circumstances that I was reunited with my family. The Jews of Bodrog-Keresztur, the village where I had been shot, were also deported to Satoraljaujhely, and the ward was always full of visitors, who had come to see the boy to whom such a miracle had happened. They all assured me that I would certainly survive the war, since Providence was evidently protecting me. Samuel Friedmann, my companion during the long walk to Bodrog-Keresztur, was one of my first visitors. He stayed at my bedside for a whole hour, his eyes filled with tears, before he spoke a word. He felt remorseful about my misfortune, because he had made me accompany him to his village. I could have reached Tokay by a shorter route, he thought. Finally, he asked me to forgive him. I told him that he was not in the least to blame for what had

69

happened. It had been God's will that I should go to Bodrog-Keresztur.

My eighty-six-year-old grandfather also came to visit me. I immediately asked him what it was that the wonder rabbi had told him about his grandson so many years before. He asked me in surprise how I knew about the matter, since he had never told anyone about it, and I related what my teacher, the wonder rabbi's son-in-law, had said to me when we took leave of each other.

The old man thought back over the years and finally remembered that my teacher had been present when the wonder rabbi had prophesied about me. Yes, it had happened exactly as my teacher had described it. My grandfather added that he had been quite confident that I would be all right when he learnt of the misfortune that had befallen me in Bodrog-Keresztur, where the wonder rabbi was buried. He had remembered the rabbi's words: 'If it should happen in this village where I shall be buried when I die, I promise you that I shall stand by him to ease his suffering.' 'I can promise you now,' said my grandfather, 'that you will certainly survive the war.'

When the gunshot wound had finally healed, even though I still could not stand on my feet because they had been so badly frozen, my family took me away from the hospital so that they could look after me themselves.

Two medical corps men put me on a stretcher and took me up to the first floor, to the little room where my brothers and sisters lived, together with some other detainees, twenty people in all. But as soon as I entered the house, my happiness at being united with my family once more began to ebb away. Instead of being overjoyed at our reunion, as I had expected them to be, my brothers and sisters ran out of the room with hunted, worried eyes.

Young Gabor, fourteen years old, was sitting on the floor, held down by two strong men, shouting and raging: 'Leave me alone! Let me go! Let me jump out of the window! I can't go on like this! I don't want to live any more!'

Distraught women were trying to talk to him and calm him down: 'Don't do anything fool-ish, Gabor. Everything will be all right, you'll see.'

Day and night Gabor used to sit by himself in a corner, crouching on the floor with his head resting on his drawn-up knees. His long, crooked nose was hidden between them, and his tousled chestnut hair, which hung down from his forehead like a curtain, shielded his face from curious glances. From his knees to his shoes his legs were streaked with tears, which poured unceasingly from his eyes. His once-white shirt was almost as black as soot. Whenever a kind-hearted woman offered him food he would push it aside with his elegant brown shoes. Now and again he would get up as quietly as a shadow, put his mouth under the tap and drink greedily. When he had had his fill of water he would creep back into his solitary corner without so much as a glance at his surroundings.

Everyone who saw the blue cross tattooed above his left knee asked the same astonished question: 'How does this Christian child come to be in the ghetto?' That it should be the fate of Jewish children to be cooped up in a ghetto was accepted almost as normal. After all, they summoned up evil spirits; they poisoned wells; they had destroyed the son of God; they denied the Prophet Mohammed. But an Aryan child who was free from all these taints? What was he doing there?

This same question had dogged Gabor ever since that Sunday morning when, dressed in his best clothes, he had attended mass—his last as it turned out—and come happily down the church steps with his school friends. As he reached the bottom, a devout gendarme who never missed mass himself called out to him: 'Now, Gabor, you come with me!'

Gabor had not the slightest inkling of how fateful

for him this summons was to be. He thought it was a good lark, and in high spirits went off side by side with the gendarme, whose son Peter was his favourite playmate. Only when he came to the big courtyard of the synagogue did he realize that this might not be such a good lark. When the wide, carved door opened before him, things looked even more serious. Then the gendarme said, and there was no jest in his voice: 'Go on, Gabor, in you go.' Gabor was thunderstruck. Struggling and writhing, he shouted: 'What have I to do in a synagogue?!'

The circumstances in which Gabor learnt of his true origins had pushed him over the edge of the abyss. He had been born in a little village, and he knew, at least by sight, all the thousand or so of his Jewish fellow villagers. He did not hate them, like all his school companions. Mr and Mrs Kovacs had not brought him up like that. Did he like Jews, though? How could he, when, day in day out, at school, in the papers, on the radio, in the streets, he heard them being cursed and derided? It can be imagined what sort of an impression the synagogue must have made on him, that same synagogue that he could see from his bedroom window. And now suddenly, here he was, shut up in the synagogue with all the Jews. A thousand pairs of eyes regarded him wonderingly. What was a Christian child doing there? Some of them perhaps were not quite so wondering. One woman, certainly, knew quite well what he was doing there. She was a midwife, and remembered perfectly well how she had delivered young Gabor fourteen years before. She had lost no time in hurrying to the registrar's office to register the birth. The entry was still there in black and white for all to see—Gabor Blumenthal, a real Jewish name.

Gabor did not have much time to look around him in the synagogue, because the heavy carved door opened once more to shouts of 'Outside! Outside!' Gabor began to breathe again. This must mean freedom, he thought. But the sight of the armed police surrounding the synagogue soon dispelled his illusion. Like everyone else, he was herded into a cattle truck and taken thirty-two miles to the ghetto.

Among the Aryan spectators standing in front of the railings round the synagogue courtyard stood a wrinkled, toothless woman, so thin that she might have been a skeleton. When she caught sight of Gabor she started to scream in despair: 'My Gabor, my most dearly beloved Gabor!' and tried to break through the police cordon to get to him. But to no avail. Mr and Mrs Kovacs were also among the bystanders and waved to Gabor to give him courage.

The boy knew the screaming woman as Aunt Marie. She was a frequent visitor at the Kovacs' house. But although Mr and Mrs Kovacs always told Gabor to be good to Aunt Marie, he could not bear her. He did not like having an aunt who looked just like a witch. The children in the street used to taunt her and call her that when she passed by. Now Gabor simply could not understand why this old witch of all people should be screaming after him in such despair.

That first day in the ghetto he was still full of hope. He was sure that there must have been some mistake and that it would soon be cleared up. His parents would soon be along to take him home. He did not move away from the window, thinking to himself every moment: 'Now they will come.' When a policeman appeared one day and asked for Gabor, he knew with certainty that the ghetto gates would soon be opened for him and he would be allowed to go free. That is what the policeman himself thought too. As he took the boy to district police headquarters he told him that his mother was waiting there to take him home.

Imagine Gabor's surprise when he entered the police building and saw, not his mother, but Aunt Marie. He had an overpowering urge to push her away when she clasped him to her with deep

75

emotion, crying: 'My dearest Gabor! My most beloved Gabor.'

Gabor had been five months old when his father
had died of pneumonia. Then his mother had become ill with tuberculosis and had been unable to
work any longer. Marie had not wanted the child
to catch the disease, so she asked the respectable and
childless Kovacs family to take him in. It had been
agreed between them that Gabor would only be
told the true facts about his birth and origins when
he reached eighteen years of age.

Now, when she saw how cold he was towards
her, Marie could not restrain herself and told him
the whole story. He stared at her in amazement, not
knowing whether to believe her or not. Marie
watched him, seeing the struggle in his mind. Then
his tears came, and she knew that he did believe her.

Gabor covered his eyes with his hands. He could
not bear to see his mother's loving glances, for he
was overcome with shame at the contempt with
which he had treated her in the past. Now, as he
looked at her between his fingers, he realized that a
mother's love was hidden behind that wrinkled
face, that a mother's heart beat in that skinny body.
When she again put her arms around him he
glowed with happiness. So did his mother, as she
felt his warm tears on her face. Then the door

opened and a police officer motioned mother and son into an adjoining room. He looked Gabor up and down, and, as soon as he saw the blue cross tattooed above his knee, asked the same question as everyone else: 'How did this Aryan child come to be in the ghetto?' Marie breathed a sigh of relief. She took Gabor's arm and prepared to leave the room with him. At first the police officer seemed perfectly willing to let them go, but just as Marie put out her hand to open the door, he changed his mind. 'Wait!' he ordered. This meant that he wanted to clear their release with a higher authority. He was a careful man and did not want to let them go solely on his own responsibility. The police officer telephoned the Gestapo chief. It soon became apparent that no permission to leave was going to be given over the telephone. This was a highly important matter of the greatest political significance. The Gestapo chief himself would take over the investigation. He would come over from chief headquarters immediately by car. Meanwhile, Gabor waited in the tender embrace of his mother for what seemed the inevitable happy ending to his tribulations.

When the elegant Gestapo officer arrived, he stood and listened attentively as the police officer gave him all the details of Gabor's case. Then,

77

stubbing out his thick cigar, he ordered Gabor to be taken out of the room. His mother followed.

The Gestapo officer went up to Gabor and began to remove the boy's trousers. Gabor was utterly amazed. What on earth was the man doing? But the officer did not stop there. The horrified boy stood as if petrified while the Gestapo man removed his underpants as well. Marie did not understand what this was all about any more than Gabor did. Then she remembered that during the First World War, customs officials used to inspect suspicious characters in this way in case they were trying to smuggle something through the customs. Then the true significance of the Gestapo man's actions dawned on her and her knees began to shake.

When, so many years ago, Marie had told her husband that she was pregnant, he had replied that, if she had a boy, he wanted him circumcised on the eighth day after his birth, as ordained by the Jewish religion. She had agreed.

She broke down completely, and crying out: 'It's all up with us now!' she collapsed. The Hungarian police officer made to come to her aid but the elegantly uniformed Gestapo man stopped him. It was all in the day's work for him to see mothers collapse in front of him. As for Gabor, he was desperately frightened and tried to jump away. But in vain. The German gave him a ringing box on the ears and told him to stand still. 'Mummy, Mummy!' cried the boy, while the Gestapo officer continued with his examination as if nothing had happened. With schoolmasterish pedantry he lectured his ignorant Hungarian colleague on the significance of circumcision and how it was a religious rite of the Jews. Only when he had finished was Gabor allowed to kneel down beside his mother who was by this time gasping for breath. On his knees beside her, Gabor saw his mother die.

He had to be torn away from his mother's body by main force and it took several armed policemen to do the job and carry him back to the ghetto.

MY GRANDFATHER

My grandfather sat by my bed the whole day, divining my slightest wish and granting it immediately.

He had spent his entire life helping the poor and the sick. He was not rich, but wealthy people used to give him money every week to enable him to keep up his charitable work.

A rich man, called Mr Engel, who lived in Tokay, was always generous where charitable enterprises were concerned. However, he did not give my grandfather a fixed amount each week, but passed across his wallet full of bank-notes for my grandfather to take as much as he needed. I was present on one occasion when my grandfather took out only one note, a 100-pengo note I think it was, from Mr Engel's wallet. 'Why don't you take it all?' I asked my grandfather. 'If I were to take it all now, how would he be able to give me anything next time?' he replied.

My grandfather had set aside one room in his house where poor people and beggars could stay overnight free of charge. The whole town called it 'the poor room'. Once a really down at heel, dirty beggar called Peter came to the house. In addition to all his other troubles, he was not quite right in the head. He liked the life in my grandfather's house so much, that he did not want to move out. He ate and drank his fill and looked on the 'poor room' as home. On one occasion, my grandmother became very angry with him because he was infesting the whole house with lice. 'I can't stand this Peter fellow any longer,' she told my grandfather. 'Since he came here the whole house has been crawling with lice.'

My grandfather laughed. 'Listen,' he said, 'and I'll tell you what happened to me once at the wonder rabbi's house in Bodrog-Keresztur.

'The rabbi, who was second to none in his love for his fellow men, put three rooms at the disposal of the poor. Anyone who wanted to could sleep, eat and drink there for as long as he liked.

'One day a dirty, neglected beggar came to the house. Like our Peter, he was infested with lice, and it was not long before the wonder rabbi's house was crawling with them. The rabbi's wife came and told him that she was not going to put up with this beggar any longer. He had infested the whole house and must be put out at once.

'Her husband replied: "If he can tolerate so many of the little creatures, surely we ought to be able to put up with the few he has passed on to us. However, if you feel that you cannot bear the situation any longer, go and get him some new clothes and ensure that he changes his underwear more often. If you do that, you can be sure that the house will soon be free of lice." The rabbi's wife bought new clothes for the beggar and the lice soon disappeared.

'You see,' concluded my grandfather, 'that was real love for one's fellow men. If you want to ensure that the house stays clean, do what the wonder rabbi's wife did and give our Peter clean underwear and clean clothes, then you can be sure that the lice will disappear.'

One day a widow from a neighbouring village came to see my grandfather in great distress. Her daughter's wedding was due to take place in a fortnight's time, she had undertaken to provide a dowry and pay for the wedding, and now she did not know where to turn to find the money. 'How much do you need?' asked my grandfather. After a little thought, the woman said 500 pengoes would be enough. 'All right,' he told her, 'go home now and come back this evening.' A few moments later my grandmother returned from doing the shopping. She already knew that grandfather had promised the widow the 500 pengoes she needed, because she had met the woman in the street and heard the whole story. 'Where are you going to get such a large sum of money?' my grandmother asked excitedly. 'Isn't it enough that you take care of our own poor and sick? Do you have to look after strangers, too? The few individuals who give you money for your charitable work will gradually tire of doing so, and the end will be that you won't be able to help the local people at all. Business is not as good now as it used to be either. Only two days ago you took up a collection for Tochmann, who is ill in hospital, and you know yourself how difficult it was to scrape together the money.'

Grandfather said nothing, but took his walking stick and went out. I followed him, because I was curious to see how the affair would turn out. He told me he was going to see Mr Engel to discuss it. As we were passing Mr Seiler's house (he had an ironmongery business) my grandfather stopped and thought about whether to call on him. He had not seen Mr Seiler in synagogue for three days now and had heard that he was ill. We went in, and Mr Seiler's son asked us to wait in the front hall for a few minutes, as the doctor, Dr Braun, was examining his father. The doctor came out shortly afterwards and said it would be advisable if nobody disturbed his patient, because he very badly needed to rest. Grandfather made to leave, but the sick man had heard his voice and called out: 'Reb Mechul, come in, will you?'

We went in and, after Mr Seiler had stopped coughing, he said: 'I had such a bad attack this morning that I thought I was finished, so I made haste to put aside a sum of money to be used for a good purpose. I have no strength left any more. Reb Mechul, will you please open the drawer of my night table and take out the envelope you'll find there. I am sure you will know how to dispose of its contents.'

Grandfather took the envelope out of the drawer. It contained no fewer than five 100-pengo notes. He wished Mr Seiler a speedy recovery and took his leave, but before he had even closed the door behind him, the sick man called out that if he did recover, he would like grandfather to return the money to him.

When we reached the street grandfather said: 'Go to the Lieber house and find the woman who came to see me. Tell her to come again, now.' I did as he told me, and the woman walked back home with me. We got there before grandfather, but he soon appeared.

He was barely inside the house when my grandmother said: 'Well, what did I tell you?'

84

'It would be better if you didn't talk quite so much,' he retorted, handing her the envelope to give to the woman.

Naturally enough, grandmother was very curious as to how grandfather had managed to obtain the money so quickly, but she did not ask, because she knew that she would not be told. Later, when we were alone, she asked me. I knew that grandfather would not want me to talk about it and did not want to tell her. But she took a sweet out of her kitchen cupboard and put it into my mouth, and I told her the whole story. 'Incredible, incredible!' was all she said.

Food was unobtainable inside the ghetto at any price. There was no ration distribution, and the reserves everyone had brought from home were dwindling. Nearly every day we used to receive food parcels from relatives and friends in Budapest. No ghetto had been set up there, so they were able to obtain food.

Most people had brought their valuables with them into the ghetto and now the Gestapo were searching for them avidly, so everyone was busy burying things in the ground.

At the beginning of May, when we had been in the ghetto about a month, two policemen appeared and told us to pack our things as we had to go with them in fifteen minutes. We asked them where they were taking us and they told us: 'To the synagogue and then to somewhere to work.'

Everybody hastened to pack up their most important belongings to take with them. Grandfather busied himself with dressing me. When he had finished, he whispered to me: 'Pull yourself together. You will come through all right.' My father hoisted me onto his shoulders and we were taken to the big synagogue, where we found thousands of other people already locked in. Everyone wanted to know where we were going, but the Hungarian soldiers who were guarding us did not know. The only German we could see was an officer, who was keeping a close watch on everything that was happening.

We sat down on the stairs leading to the women's gallery, while grandfather told us stories about children who had given their lives for their religion. By the time he started to tell us about Hannah and her seven sons, several dozen children had gathered round. Wiping his tears away with his handkerchief, he began:

'More that two thousand years ago, when Palestine was occupied by foreigners, their princes wanted to force the Jews to worship their alien gods. The Emperor sent for Hannah and her seven sons, who were all known for their piety. In the presence of the princes, the Emperor commanded Hannah's oldest son to bow down before the alien gods. The young man refused because, he said, God's First Commandment, given at Sinai, declared: "I am the Lord, your God." The Emperor had him killed. The second son also refused to bow down before the Emperor's gods, because the Ten Commandments said: "Thou shalt not worship any strange gods." He, too, was killed.

'All Hannah's seven sons refused to obey the Emperor's command, and all of them were killed. The youngest was only three years old and the Emperor wanted to spare him, even though he had refused to kneel before the idols. "I shall throw down a ring before the wooden god," he told the child, "and I want you to bend down and pick it up, so that all the princes will see and think that you have bowed down before the idol. If you do this, you will be spared." The little boy replied: "If you, who are a human being of flesh and blood, think so highly of your honour, then it is certainly my duty to esteem the honour of the Almighty, who created heaven and earth." The Emperor commanded that he, too, be put to death.

'Hannah, his mother, who had already seen six of

her sons killed, asked the Emperor that she be allowed to embrace her youngest son and kiss him just once before he was put to death. Her request was granted. After she had embraced him and kissed him, she said: "My child, tell our forefather Abraham that he erected an altar to sacrifice one son for God, but I have erected seven altars and sacrificed seven sons." Then she climbed onto a nearby roof, threw herself off and died.'

We were apparently going to be sent somewhere in southern Hungary to do forced labour. My father was worried about me. Those who were fit, he thought to himself, would get by somehow, but the arduous journey into the unknown might spell the end for the sick. Although the inmates of the ghetto were forbidden to have any money and were supposed to have handed over any they might have possessed when they were herded into the ghetto, my father had secreted some on him and now he pulled a bundle of notes out of his pocket and gave it to a Hungarian officer, asking him to see that I was taken to the ghetto hospital, which was not far away. The officer put the money away, lifted me onto his shoulder and took me to the hospital himself.

'You will have to make room for this boy,' the

co-operative Hungarian officer told a nurse at the hospital.

'But where shall we put him? We haven't got a single empty bed,' she complained.

'I don't care what you do, but you've got to make room for him,' the Hungarian retorted. The nurse cleared a space for me on the floor and I lay down, a myriad thoughts racing through my head. Were they really taking everyone off to work for them? They couldn't be, otherwise why were they taking old people and babies as well? Babies couldn't work; nor could eighty- and ninety-year-olds. A horrifying thought struck me. Were they going to kill everyone? The more I tried to dismiss the thought, the more certain I became that I had hit on the truth. Was I to be the only member of my family to survive? What meaning would life have for me then? I must go with my family, whatever Fate might have in store for them. 'Nurse, nurse!' I called at the top of my voice. She hurried over to me.

'Where do you think you are?' she said furiously. 'This isn't a public-house, you know. What do you mean by shouting like that?' Her scolding went in one ear and out of the other.

'Please, please let me out of here. I want to go back to the synagogue. I must go with my parents!'

'Don't talk nonsense. Anyone else would be overjoyed at the chance of being in hospital. Be content and praise God that you are one of the lucky ones.'

'Please, nurse, please. There is no time now for long discussions. Find a soldier and get him to take me back to my family.'

'Do you think I have soldiers under my command and can order one to take you to the synagogue just like that? They have their own commanders. They are not here just to be at your beck and call.'

I lost my temper at this. 'I want to go with my parents!' I raged. 'I will not stay here, do you hear me, I will not stay here!' Everyone came running as I screamed and shouted.

A Hungarian soldier rushed over to see what was the matter. 'He's gone mad,' the nurse told him, 'he wants to go back to the synagogue, to his parents.'

'So he shall then,' replied the soldier. He picked me up like a sack of potatoes and carried me the two hundred yards or so to the synagogue. But my family were nowhere to be seen. They had already gone.

But I had no time to consider my new situation. A powerful pair of hands seized me and threw me bodily into a horse-box. Next to me sat a blind old man, calling out over and over again for his daughter. 'Esther, Esther, where are you? Why has she left me alone like this?' After a quarter of an hour, the horse-box drew up in a field outside the town, surrounded by S.S. men. They forced us out of the horse-box and shoved us into a waiting train of cattle-trucks, eighty people to a truck. There was hardly room to sit down and the atmosphere was suffocating, because the tiny windows had to remain bolted shut—those were the orders. I forgot my own misery in the crying of thirsty children, the groans of sick people in pain and the death rattle of the dying. A five-year-old child kept asking his father: 'Daddy, where are we going?'

Patiently his father replied: 'To heaven, son, to heaven.'

'You have always said that Grannie is in heaven, are we going to see her?'

'Yes, we are going to see her.'

'God lives in heaven, doesn't he? Are we going to see him as well?'

'Yes, of course.'

'Is there a children's room there for me and for Kathi?'

'Oh yes, there is a very nice children's room.'

'I would like to have a room for myself, because Kathi is always taking my toys. I will keep my room locked and won't let her in again.'

'Well then, I won't lend you my doll any more,' said Kathi.

'I won't need your doll. There are plenty of little angels in heaven for me to play with.'

'Oh, mummy, are all the angels just for him? He is so selfish, he wants everything for himself.'

'It's all right,' said Kathi's mother. 'There will be enough for both of you and for the other children, too.'

Nobody in the railway truck realized that for most of its occupants there would be no return from their journey. When the train crossed the Hungarian frontier and entered Poland many of us began to feel uneasy, because we had been assured that we were being sent to southern Hungary. But Jews have always tended to be optimists, and all sorts of explanations were soon forthcoming. 'Probably the lines have been damaged, so they have to send us to southern Hungary via Poland,' somebody suggested. The train had been travelling northwards and when it turned westwards many of those in the cattle-trucks saw this as confirmation of their optimistic explanations. I was perhaps the only person in the train who had even the slightest idea of what awaited us all, since I had already had a certain amount of experience of the Nazis. However, I kept my forebodings to myself.

Gabor travelled with me in the cattle-truck. He seemed to have recovered from his first shock, and was intensely interested in learning Hebrew so that he could begin to understand something of the religion of his forebears. I had a prayer-book with me and began to give him instruction. Before many hours had passed, Gabor could already recite a short prayer in Hebrew.

Nevertheless, he had no intention of giving up his Christian beliefs. 'I want to be a good Christian as well as a good Jew,' he said, not once but many times. In the mornings, he knelt and said his Christian prayers, and then stood up and said the Hebrew ones.

He had many plans for later life. In his view, mankind's whole misfortune lay in the schisms between all the various religions. Although they all preached love of one's neighbour, high moral and ethical standards, and so on, none practised these qualities towards each other. Gabor was in the process of formulating a plan whereby all the religions of the world could be united into one, thus bringing peace and unity to all the warring factions of mankind.

Nevertheless, he saw that it might well be impossible to reconcile the different conceptions embodied in such religions as Buddhism, Islam and so on. Each had its own idea of God, sometimes mutually contradictory. 'Oh, you Gods, why don't you join forces!' he used to shout in despair.

93

ON THE THRESHOLD OF
THE GAS CHAMBER

After three days the train stopped. It was midnight, and we had reached our destination. As the first glimmers of light seeped into the truck, the doors were flung open.

'Everybody out, everybody out! Leave all your things in the railway wagons!' As the shouted orders assailed us from every direction, the stronger ones among us jumped out of the wagons, while the old and the weak pulled themselves slowly and painfully to their feet and prepared to climb out as well. Young mothers picked their babies up in their arms. I, too, tried to stand up and, miracle of miracles, I found that I could. For the first time since I had been shot and wounded I was able to stand on my own two feet. I attempted to take a few steps, and found that I could walk as well. I was the last to leave the by now empty wagon, empty of the living that is, for there were more than a few dead bodies lying on the floor.

A big board on a pole told us where we were. AUSCHWITZ, it proclaimed in large letters. As I saw the name, I came over faint. I remembered a young woman who had managed to flee to Hungary from Poland six months before. She hid herself away in the synagogue cellars, and I took her food three times a day. She did not stop talking about Auschwitz, Maidanek and Treblinka the whole time. Everyone there had been gassed and their bodies burnt, she said. We all thought she was mad at the time, but now, here we were at Auschwitz. When I saw the name-board, I began to believe what the young woman from Poland had said. But only for a few moments. 'No, it can't be true,' I muttered to myself. 'How can it be true, when grandfather promised me that I would survive?'

To right and left, in front and behind, barbed wire fences stretched away unendingly. At intervals along them were watch-towers. Dozens and dozens of busy soldiers went purposefully about their business. They relieved each other on duty, gave orders, received them and carried them out, quietly and peacefully. But, despite the calm atmosphere, Mr Klein was murmuring the 'Vidu', the prayer before death.

Not far away, thick black smoke belched skywards from an unusually tall chimney. As the smoke dispersed, the beams of the sun broke through it, giving it a golden glow, and then the wind carried

95

it away over our heads. The smoke smelt of burning flesh.

But the polite way we were told to enter separately, men together and women together, stilled any forebodings. After all, if everything was on such a high moral level, how could anything wicked be going on?

A long column of marching men in blue-striped uniforms came in sight. The man in charge wore the same uniform. We knew that he was in charge because he held a swagger stick in his right hand. With a blast on his whistle he brought the column sharply to a halt, the uniformed men with their close-cropped hair bringing their heels smartly together as they obeyed the command. Another blast on the whistle, and the men dispersed, running towards the empty cattle-trucks. Soon trunks, boxes, bundles and even bodies began flying out of the wagons onto the concrete platforms.

One of the uniformed men ran up to me, looked to right and left, and then tapped me on the shoulder. Putting his mouth against my ear, he whispered: 'You are eighteen years old.' Before I could ask him what he meant, he turned and ran off so quickly that he was lost to sight in a flash.

At that moment I caught sight of my mother standing with all the other women, and choked back the cry that came to my lips. She was doing what every good mother does in trying circumstances, soothing her hungry, thirsty, tired children. What a godsend that I did not know then that I was seeing her for almost the last time! And how happy I would be now to know for certain that she was entirely unaware of the fact that she was not long for this world.

As I looked away again, I saw a very tall S.S. man in immaculate uniform standing some distance away. His feet were spread wide apart and he held his hands behind his back. Gabor was standing in front of him and he was looking at the boy with obvious puzzlement. What was this fair-haired, Aryan-looking boy doing here, with a yellow star sewn on the breast of his jacket? As the S.S. man's gaze travelled downwards, he was still more puzzled to see the cross tattooed on Gabor's thigh.

'What's wrong with you? What are you, a Jew or a Christian?' Gabor did not understand a word of German, but he guessed what the S.S. man was saying to him.

'Yes,' he shouted in Hungarian, 'you are surprised, aren't you! I'm both, I'm a Jew and a Christian.' The S.S. man motioned with his gloved hand, calling over another officer who spoke Hungarian. Again Gabor shouted in Hungarian that he was a

Jew and a Christian and that he wanted to remain so.

Seeing that the Gestapo man was still not completely convinced, Gabor pointed downwards to his loins. 'You can see for yourself, if you want to,' he yelled. The Gestapo man believed him then, and motioned him to the left. Staring at the smoking chimney. Gabor started to walk off. I wonder what thoughts went through his head in the last few seconds before he faced his inescapable fate.

'How old are you,' the S.S. man asked Mr Klein, who was standing immediately in front of me. 'Fifty-five,' he answered. 'To the left,' said the S.S. man. As I heard the question and answer, it was borne in on me that a prisoner's age must have some special significance, since the tall S.S. man was asking everyone how old they were. Now it was my turn to stand before him. He looked me up and down and then asked me the inevitable question: 'Well, and how old are you?' It was on the tip of my tongue to tell the truth and say, 'Sixteen,' but as he asked me again with menace in his voice, I stammered, 'Eighteen.' 'To the right,' the S.S. man said.

At that precise moment I saw my mother again. She had been sent to the left and had already moved forward quite a distance. A powerful feeling urged

98

me to join her, and instead of going to the right, as I had been ordered to do, I went to the left. But I had only taken two or three steps when I felt strong hands seize me by the collar and drag me back to the right. I turned round and looked at the S.S. man, but he was already busy with those behind me in the queue and had no glances to spare for me.

The long line moved slowly forward and I with it. Suddenly, somebody called my name. I looked round and saw my father. 'What are you doing here?' he asked. 'I thought you were safely out of it.' I told him what had happened. 'You shouldn't be here. You were safe in the hospital, but here . . . Oh, what a shame, what a shame,' my father said.

We were pushed into an enormous hut. 'Undress except for your shoes and leave your clothes on the floor. See that you do it in orderly fashion, trousers in one pile, jackets in another, shirts in another!' As we obeyed the shouted orders, barbers, who were standing ready, gave us a close crop and shaved off our body hair. Then, naked, we were marched off to another huge building with the word 'Showers' over the entrance.

'Comrades,' shouted a short, fat man, who was visibly scared, 'don't believe it. This is no shower-bath. Even if it looks like one, it isn't. It's the place where we shall all be asphyxiated.' He had fled to

Hungary from Poland, and he had heard of shower-baths where poison gas flowed from the showers, not hot water.

My heart was beating fit to burst as I stood under the shower. I felt as a man condemned to death must feel when he steps onto the gallows. As I waited for the gas to come pouring out of the shower, I felt something warm on my head. It was hot water. This shower-bath, at least, was a real one. Was the Pole wrong, then? No, he was all too right. Water was flowing from these showers, it is true, but, in the building topped by that gigantic chimney there, 'Showers' was also written over the entrance. But the showers did not release hot water over the people standing beneath them, they released poison gas. The Pole knew what he was talking about.

Soon we were dressed in our blue-striped uniforms, the uniforms of slavery. It must have been long after midnight when we were ordered to line up in fives in the darkness, shivering with cold. It took all my strength to stand on my feet. My ears were buzzing and my knees shaking. My thin body was too heavy for them. As my eye-lids began to close, a thunderous crash forced them open again. The whole area was lit up by an enormous sheet of flame which seemed to reach from the ground right up into the sky. Everyone stared at the leaping flames, wondering what had caused them. 'There go your old clothes,' said the German soldiers. No one had asked them and they did not usually volunteer information.

'What a shocking waste,' somebody exclaimed, although we could not make out who.

'What!' roared one of the guards, 'do you think Germans would want to wear your lousy clothes!' But it was not our clothes that were burning. I did not know it then, thank God, but it was the bodies of our loved ones.

After a while we were pushed into a hut, and so tightly were we packed together that it was impossible even to sit down. Everybody slept standing up, wedged against one another like sardines in a tin. Only at dawn, when the prisoners rushed out on parade, was it possible to lie down, but then there was no time. We had to fall in outside for physical jerks. 'Knees bend! Knees stretch! Arms stretch! Arms bend!' An S.S. man came and counted us and then we had to do more physical jerks. After this, post-cards were distributed. They were for us to send to those of our relatives who were still in Hungary. We had to say how wonderful conditions were in the camp, so that they would feel no fear when their turn came to be deported.

The block senior made a little speech. 'It is not true that people are gassed and burnt here. That is enemy atrocity propaganda.' I believed him. And I believed him when he said that old people and children were put on 'light work' like basket-weaving. The thought occurred to me that, since my hands were useless as a result of having been frozen, and since my feet pained me, it would be better if I, too, could do light work.

'Mr Block Senior,' I begged, 'I cannot do heavy work because of my hands, please let me go with the old people and the children.' Two ringing blows on the side of my head were the answer to my plea. I fell to the ground. Only much later, when I knew what had happened to the old people and children sent to Auschwitz and other camps, did I realize that the block senior's blows were a blessing in disguise. I owed my life to them.

Camp rules laid it down that newly arrived prisoners received no food for the first two days. Some said this was to prevent any attempts at revolt, others that it was meant to be our first 'act of atonement'. In any event, we had our first food on our third day in Auschwitz, thick soup dished out in buckets, one bucket to ten prisoners. I could not bring myself to have any of the soup. Not only did prisoners have to lap it up with their tongues and mouths like pigs at a trough, for there were no spoons, but the buckets the soup was distributed in were the same buckets in which we had to relieve ourselves.

We did not have to work, and despite the hours of physical jerks, there was still plenty of time to sit about the camp compound and watch the thousands of newcomers arriving at the camp every day. The routine never varied. It was always the same down to the last tiny detail. Most of the new arrivals were sent to the left, only a few to the right.

One day I saw an old school companion of mine, Mandel, on the other side of the barbed wire. He had just arrived with the second contingent of Jews from Satoraljaujhely. He told me that everyone in the hospital, including doctors and nurses, had been sent to the gas chambers. Then I realized how 'safe' I would have been in the hospital. Once again, I had been saved by a miracle.

MAUTHAUSEN

I think I spent about ten days in Auschwitz, my mind in utter confusion the whole time. Not only did I have no idea what day it was, but I was not even sure whether it was morning, afternoon or night-time. Time seemed to be standing still, and that is why I do not know exactly how long I was there. It could not have been more than ten days, however. Then we were put into cattle-trucks again and sent to the camp at Mauthausen.

When we arrived at our destination, S.S. men escorted us to the camp. The concentration camp at Mauthausen lay on a hill, and it had been sited in such a way that it was invisible from below. From the outside, the camp looked like a fortress. Above the broad entrance gate was a large observation post where a number of S.S. men kept watch on all who went in or out. We had a bad moment as we were about to march through the gate. Our guards released the safety catches on their weapons, and we thought they were going to open fire, but apparently they were just warning us not to try any tricks.

The first building on the right inside the gate was a shower block. Great stress was laid on cleanliness at Mauthausen. Every prisoner had to have a thorough shower and was then issued with clean clothes and underwear. After we had had a shower we were lined up outside again and divided up into groups. My brother and cousin happened to be standing some way away from me, so they were put into a different group and marched off to another camp. Mauthausen consisted of a complex of camps, and as deportees arrived from Auschwitz they were allocated to the various camps according to need.

The group I was in was marched off to a barrack block where we were told that we would be quarantined for eight days. During that time we did not have to work at all and we had no feeling that we were shut up in what was, in fact, the most barbarous camp of them all. We could not see what was going on elsewhere, since we were locked into our barrack block. Because I was a youngster, the block senior was particularly considerate. He gave me an extra ration of soup every day and told me stories about his experiences during the three years he had spent in Mauthausen. It was like a sanatorium now, he said, compared with what it had been like earlier. When I asked him for details, he told me:

'I used to be a Kapo (camp policeman) and have to take a hundred men out to work every day. At the gate I was told how many I was to bring back alive that evening, and come what might I had to ensure that the figure was not exceeded. It varied from day to day, but I always had to kill at least five, and when they started sending Russian prisoners to Mauthausen, I often had to kill as many as fifty. Only one man ever tried to resist, a Russian who was said to have been an officer. He went for me one day and would have killed me if the S.S. had not come to my assistance. They grabbed him and set their dogs on him.'

'Isn't it on your conscience that you have killed so many people?' I asked him.

'They would have been killed just the same. If I hadn't done it, somebody else would have, or the S.S. themselves would have finished them off.'

I asked him why he was in Mauthausen and he told me that he had stabbed his wife to death. She was a 'miserable bitch', he said, who had been unfaithful to him many times. When he had caught her with one of her lovers, he had knifed her and been sentenced to life imprisonment. That had been in 1940. A year later he had been sent from prison to Mauthausen.

'One day,' he recounted, 'the prison governor came and told me that someone important had come to visit me. I wondered who it could be,

106

because I had never had a visitor before, not even my relatives. In any case, it was not a visiting day. When I asked the governor who had come to see me, he told me that it was the Gestapo. My heart started pounding. What did the Gestapo want with me? The governor took me into his office, where two Gestapo men were waiting for me. They greeted me in a friendly enough manner and gave me a cigarette.

' "How are you?" one of them asked me. "As well as can be expected for a convict," I told him. "How would you like to be better off?" "Very much." "Are you a nationalist?" I wasn't one, of course, but said that I was. "The Third Reich has many enemies," the Gestapo man continued, "and now the time of reckoning has come. We need energetic people who will have the courage to deal with these enemies and teach them a lesson. Are you prepared to do such work?"

'I told him I was, so they gave me a packet of cigarettes and left, saying that they would be coming back for me. They did so a few days later and took me to Dachau as a Kapo. After a few months, I was sent to Mauthausen and here I am.'

He knew that I could not do heavy work, but he told me not to have any illusions. Anyone at Mauthausen who could not work was killed.

MELK

When the eight-day quarantine period was over we were again put on a train. When it drew up at a small station, I looked out of the window and saw the name of the place on a big board. MELK, it said. I had never heard the name before, but some of my companions had passed through it by car or train in happier days.

The platform was filled with soldiers armed with machine-guns. It was, in the circumstances, a pleasant surprise to see that they did not have the lightning-flash insignia of the S.S. on their collars. We all felt that ordinary troops would treat us better than the S.S. had done, although only time would tell whether we were correct. But still, even the smallest glimmer of hope served to raise our depressed and wretched spirits, even if it should later turn out to be illusory.

The station was cleared of civilians, and then we heard the by now familiar order: 'Everybody out, everybody out.' Slowly we climbed down onto the platform. This time we had not been crowded into cattle-trucks, but had travelled in first-class coaches, a fact that had cheered the more optimistic among us. It must mean that our situation was going to improve, and even if this should later turn out to be a false hope, at least we had lost nothing. It had been so pleasant to live under a beautiful illusion for an hour.

'Stretch your arms sideways and fall in five deep!' came the command. We obeyed automatically, because we had had to do this parade drill twenty times a day in the camps. After counting us to make sure nobody was missing, our escorts took up position to the right and left of us and we were ordered to march off. As we left the station they cocked their pistols. We knew what this meant. Anyone attempting to escape would be shot immediately. Whether anyone actually had any thought of trying to escape is doubtful, because we were very closely guarded indeed. Apart from that, where could any of us escape to? We were in a foreign country and we were dressed in striped prison clothes.

As we marched along we saw women with shopping bags going to the shops. They glared at us with contempt and hatred and we could see what they were thinking: 'There they go, the stinking rabble. They wanted the war! They are responsible for the air-raids on our cities. Well, good. They'll soon be singing a different tune in the concentration camp!'

Two eight-year-olds came along the road with

their school satchels. 'Look, Fritz,' one of them called out to his friend, pointing at us with an accusing finger, 'look at this dirty lot. They're the worst criminals there are, enemies of the Fuehrer and the German Reich. Now our soldiers are taking them to the concentration camp. They will be well and truly beaten there.'

It was a glorious spring day, and the blossoming fruit trees transformed the landscape into a veritable picture. But all this only served to depress me more. I looked up at the sun, shining down so brightly from the sky, and thought to myself: How can you look on and do nothing, while we are being plagued and persecuted down here on earth? An old peasant went by, driving a cow before him. What a fortunate animal! Oh God, if you would only turn me into a happy, peaceful creature like that cow. She doesn't know how lucky she is. Nobody persecutes her, nobody maltreats her. Why aren't we asked what we want to be born as before we come into the world? And when we are born, we do not know why or how or to what end.

As soon as we can say a few words, we have to learn to hold a fork properly, behave ourselves like good boys and girls, keep our clothes clean. At five or six we go to school. We learn our alphabet, our two times table. Our teachers tell us all the time how wonderful Hungary is. It is the most beautiful, noble and honourable country in the world. Hungarian soldiers are the best in the world. The greatest honour any man can have is to die for his fatherland. We are taught about the great Hungarian patriot and poet, Petöfi, and the thousands like him who gladly shed their noble blood for the fatherland, Hungary. We sing the national anthem on every conceivable festive occasion. By the time we leave school we, too, are patriots, prepared, if need be, to sacrifice our lives for our country. We are ready to be soldiers and obey whatever commands our officers give us. We know, because that is what our teachers have hammered into our heads, that there is no more glorious death than to die fighting for Hungary. And then, suddenly, Hungarian soldiers wearing the beloved, the glorious uniform of our fatherland, take us, throw us into cattle-trucks and send us off to a foreign country, telling the Germans who await us, the Germans who were always held up to us as an example, 'Here, take them. Do what you like with them!'

The president of our community, Mr Frankel, considered it of over-riding importance that we should be given our religious instruction in correct German. 'How can one become a cultured person, if one does not know German?' he used to say.

My religion teacher's German was not perfect, so he had to give us our lessons with a German Bible in his hand, so that he could refer to it and not, heaven forbid, use any expression that was not grammatically correct. Poor man, he was always having his faulty German thrown up in his face, and feared for his job because of it. Once, when he made some small mistake during an examination, there was a scandal. Some people even demanded that he be dismissed out of hand. Only the fact that he had nine children saved him, but he had to promise to take lessons from a private language teacher.

We were always being told to be polite, like the Germans. Now I could see how they behaved, these polite, cultured Germans, who were always being held up as examples of perfection. They persecuted and maltreated us and would not leave us in peace.

We reached the camp gate. A painted notice board met our eyes, with the legend: 'WARNING! CONCENTRATION CAMP! ANYONE LOITERING NEAR THIS ENTRANCE WILL BE SHOT!' To emphasize the message, a skull and crossbones had been painted above it. We had to wait half an hour before the order came to march into the camp. We marched past a barracks and then came to a second gate. This was the camp itself, and our new home.

We looked about us to see what it was like. What we saw were a few barrack blocks surrounded by two electrified barbed wire fences. In the space between the fences were watch-towers set twenty yards apart, every one with machine-guns trained on the camp.

There were flowers and fruit trees, too, so that a stranger visiting the camp might well have believed that here was a modern penal establishment aimed not at punishing, but at rehabilitating the inmates.

We were mustered on the so-called parade ground, ready for the camp commandant to come and receive us himself. At least an hour went by before the gate was opened to admit the great man. We were loudly called to attention. Everybody in the camp, soldiers as well as prisoners, had to stand stiffly to attention whenever the commandant appeared.

As always, he was accompanied by his body-guard, a six-foot adjutant. He was no longer a young man. In fact, he appeared to be well over sixty. He did not look a wicked man at all, but his bodyguard did. The adjutant pulled up a chair and the commandant climbed onto it to address us.

'Prisoners! In case any of you are not sure where you are, I'll tell you. This is a concentration camp. And for whom have concentration camps been set up? For the parasites and common criminals who have set the world on fire. We did not have to bring you here. We have the power to shoot you like mad dogs. Nobody can stop us. But we want to give you another chance. It's a slim one, true, but it's still a chance. Your chance lies in work, for through work you will be able to prove that you repent of your misdeeds and are ready to pay for your sins. Anybody who is work-shy, and I know that means most of you, will be ruthlessly punished, because we have no room here for people who don't earn their daily bread. The slogan here is: "Work for bread, and bread for work" and don't you forget it.'

His adjutant helped him down from the chair and climbed onto it himself in order to read out some of the more important camp regulations.

'Anyone refusing to obey an order will be shot.'

'Anyone attempting to escape, helping someone else to attempt to escape, or withholding information about an intended escape attempt, will be shot.'

'Anyone attempting to commit sabotage will be shot.'

Then came some less onerous regulations dealing with offences meriting floggings of from twenty-five to a hundred lashes. All Kapos were authorized to award a flogging and carry it out, and there was

114

no appeal against it. The prisoner being flogged must freely submit to being punished and do everything in his power to ensure that the punishment was administered without any hitch whatever.

Penalties were designed to assist in the rehabilitation of prisoners and must be regarded in this light. They should not be considered as mistreatment, because prisoners were never mistreated in concentration camps.

Then he shouted: 'All rabbis step forward.' Although there were many rabbis in our group, nobody stepped forward. Even when the adjutant offered to ensure them special treatment, nobody identified himself as a rabbi. Then the adjutant offered an extra loaf of bread to anyone pointing out a rabbi, but still nobody moved.

Later, one of the old-timers explained that 'special treatment' in concentration camp jargon meant death by hanging.

When we were dismissed and sent to our barrack block, the block senior regarded us with scorn. 'Now then, you lot. Have a good look round. This is your block. Don't forget to keep it clean, because it's your home. The whip reigns supreme here. Take a good look at it,' and he held it up for us all to see.

'This whip works wonders,' he continued. 'It

makes good, obedient people out of the most undisciplined individuals. It is also successful as a weight reducer for obese directors, bankers, lawyers and businessmen. In short, this whip is a panacea for all ills.

'As you already know, the minimum punishment is twenty-five lashes on your backside. If I award you twenty-five lashes—now make a note of this—you will drop your trousers and pants and bend down until your finger-tips touch your toenails. You will hold this position until the last stroke. If you move, we start again from number one. The prisoner being flogged is obliged to count the number of lashes loudly and clearly.

'And now, just to give you a taste of the educational power of the whip, every one of you will receive five lashes immediately. Don't regard it as punishment but as an introduction. All right, strip!'

He lined up about ten Kapos with whips and we all had the choice of whom we wanted to administer the whipping. I chose the Kapo who looked the weakest of the bunch. But the first stroke of the whip showed me that I had erred.

As soon as the whipping was over, we thought that we would be left alone, but we were wrong. The next item on the agenda was the so-called lice inspection. This was nothing new to us, because we had already been subjected to it at Mauthausen. This hateful and degrading procedure was carried out as follows:

Prisoners stripped and handed over their clothes for inspection to one of the barrack orderlies. Meanwhile, the block senior seated himself on a chair and placed a footstool in front of him. Then the naked prisoners stood in a row and mounted the footstool one by one. The block senior sat on his chair like an oriental chieftain on a throne, a short wooden stick the thickness and size of a pencil in his hand. As each prisoner stepped in front of him, the block senior gestured with his stick. This meant: Raise your right arm. Then the block senior dug his fingers into the prisoner's armpit to see if there were any lice there. Another wave of the stick meant: Raise your left arm. When the block senior tapped the prisoner's leg he had to climb onto the footstool facing the block senior, who then examined his private parts. Another tap, and the prisoner had to turn round and bend over while the block senior continued his examination. One last tap with the stick was the signal for dismissal. If however, instead of a tap, a prisoner received a kick in the behind, this meant a flogging from one of the waiting Kapos for being lousy or dirty. In fact a prisoner might be perfectly clean, but if the block senior thought he deserved a flogging for any reason at all —or for no reason—he just intimated that the prisoner was lousy or dirty.

After a prisoner had been whipped he was allowed to go to the wash-room and wash himself thoroughly before presenting himself for inspection again. Any prisoner unfortunate enough not to pass this second inspection would be taken into the ablution room and literally scrubbed raw with a hard scrubbing brush. Few survived this treatment.

The lice inspection over, we were given a ration of bread and some blackish water which was supposed to be coffee. It tasted like rancid soap-suds, but at least it warmed one's inside.

Finally we lay down on our bunks, but it was strictly forbidden to keep our shoes on or take them into our bunks. They had to be put underneath, on the floor. Obediently, I put my good shoes and the warm socks my mother had knitted for me in the Satoraljaujhely ghetto under my bunk and fell into a deep sleep.

At four o'clock in the morning, we were all awakened by an ear-splitting whistle, followed by shouts of 'Get up!' The block senior ran from bunk to bunk, using his club on anybody who had not leapt out the moment the whistle sounded.

Each bunk had to be made up in the precise

manner prescribed by camp regulations, and any deviation was very severely punished. I could still not use my hands properly, so I asked my neighbour to make up my bunk for me, which he did. Then I bent down to look for my shoes and found to my horror that they were gone. I searched everywhere, but could find no trace of them. I was by no means the only prisoner without shoes, although this was small consolation. One rumour that soon went round was that the block senior had told all his friends in the other blocks to come and steal any good shoes they could find while we were asleep. Another version was that the block senior himself was the thief and had bartered our shoes with the troops for brandy. The troops sold the shoes on the black market. This suspicion was strengthened when the block senior was seen to be hiding a big hoard of brandy under his bunk.

There was an enormous queue for the latrines, where the 'Scheissmeister' (excrement master), as he was called, kept order with a heavy club, admitting only as many as came out. Once inside, one could not dawdle. Another 'Scheissmeister' inside lashed at anyone he thought was taking too long. The only thing to do then was to rejoin the queue. The cleverer prisoners used to get up an hour before the whistle sounded in order to beat the rush to the latrines, but soon, so many were getting up early that they defeated their own purpose.

After the latrines came the coffee distribution and then the roll-call. First we had to line up outside our block, where the block senior counted us. When the figure tallied we had to move off at the double to the big parade-ground, where the prisoners from the whole camp had to assemble to be counted. As soon as all were present, the commandant himself appeared, to conduct the roll-call in person.

When all the figures tallied, it did not take long, and the prisoners were marched off to work. Great emphasis was laid on soldierly bearing at the camp roll-call. Woe betide anyone who was slovenly in his movements or did not stand stiffly to attention. The commandant, the highest being in the world of the concentration camp, who had the power of life and death over all the inmates, insisted that they, his minions, be soldierly in their bearing at all times. He had an eagle eye for any irregularity and was quick to pounce on it. Any prisoner who did not come up to standard was shot.

Should any prisoner be too weak to drag himself to the parade-ground, the Kapos and block seniors would themselves take him there and then beat him up while everyone looked on, 'pour encourager les autres'. It often happened that a prisoner who wished to die deliberately absented himself from the roll-call. Such prisoners could be certain that their wish would be granted.

The roll-call over, we were marched off to work. The gate was opened, and we passed through it onto the road, which was under repair and covered with small, sharp stones. We were accompanied by a posse of guards armed with machine-guns, and proceeded at the double. Anyone who could not keep up was helped along with a gun butt. Since I had no shoes, the stones cut into my feet at every step, but I had no time to think about them because I was too busy keeping up with my companions. After one and a half miles at the double we reached a deserted piece of ground by the railway, where the cattle-trucks were drawn up ready to take us to our place of work. In the few seconds before we were pushed into the trucks, I examined my feet and saw that they were very badly cut and bleeding.

After counting us once again, the guards forced us into the waiting cattle-trucks, cramming us in like sardines. So tightly did they wedge us into the trucks, that some prisoners either suffocated or were crushed to death by the time we arrived at our destination, fifteen minutes later.

When we got out of the train at our destination,

we were counted again and then divided up into several groups, because there were several work sites fairly close to each other. The group I was in consisted of about a hundred men. We were marched to our place of work about three hundred yards away and set about our job, which was to carry bags of cement from a huge pile to a building site a hundred yards or so further on. Since my hands were more or less useless, I could not load a bag of cement onto my shoulders by myself, but had to ask one of my fellow prisoners to do it for me. Then I was faced with another problem—how to prevent the bag from sliding off my shoulders to the ground. I could not hold it because of my hands, so I stooped forward and tried desperately to carry the cement balanced across my shoulders. My efforts were in vain. After a few steps, down crashed the bag onto the ground and burst open. My comrades hurriedly tried to dispose of the torn bag and cover up the cement scattered all over the ground before the Kapo spotted it, since he was some distance away. Our luck was out, however. One of the guards saw what had happened and called the Kapo over. 'Look what this swine has done!' he shouted, as the Kapo came towards me in a rage. The civilian foreman started across to us as well, to see what all the fuss was about.

For a split second I wondered whether I ought to explain about my hands, but remembered that the old-timers had often warned me against disclosing that my hands were useless, so I kept quiet. Prisoners who were unable to work were not tolerated, or even punished. They were liquidated.

The Kapo and the foreman were holding a discussion about the heinous crime I had committed. The Kapo, who wore a green star on his uniform to show that he was a convicted murderer, was of the opinion that what I had done was a clear case of sabotage and deserved to be punished by death. The foreman, on the other hand, thought that the law permitted my youth to be considered an extenuating circumstance and that a lesser sentence was in order. Moreover, this was my first offence, so they would be justified in awarding me a lighter sentence. I ought to be given twenty-five lashes, said the foreman. The Kapo thought this not severe enough, but agreed to twenty-five lashes when the soldier who had called him over joined in the discussion to shout, 'Yes, yes, twenty-five lashes on the arse, that's what he deserves.' At this the foreman went back to his job.

Rubbing his hands together in gleeful anticipation, the Kapo prepared to carry out the sentence on the spot. But first he would have to run back to the camp to fetch his whip. The heavy club he carried was not adequate to the task he had in mind.

He soon returned and, knowing I was new in the camp, asked me if I knew the regulations concerning floggings. I said I did. He told me to bend over, raised his whip and, before the first blow fell, told me that I ought to be happy at being awarded such mild punishment. I suppose I ought to have been, because it might have been appreciably worse. However, all I could think about when the whip came down was how long this agony was going to last.

I counted the strokes out loud as the regulations demanded, groaning with pain and with stars flashing before my eyes. At last, I reached twenty-five and thought my ordeal was at an end. But no. One of the civilian building workers, fresh to the job probably, had watched the flogging and apparently derived a great deal of pleasure from it, for he came over now and asked if he could try his hand at handing out a whipping. His actual words were: 'I'd like to take a few cracks at this enemy swine's arse.' The Kapo did not answer at first, but when the labourer repeated his request, the Kapo gave him the whip and told him to 'have a try, then'. As for me, I did not even wait for the Kapo to order me to bend over, but took up the prescribed stance

124

straight away. The civilian worker roared with laughter.

'Aren't they wonderfully trained,' he shouted. 'They get ready to be flogged without even being told to.'

'Yes,' said the Kapo, 'the whip is a marvellous way of educating people.'

Racked with pain, I staggered back to the heap of cement bags. It was impossible to try and carry any more cement now, because if I dropped another bag, it would be all up with me. I decided to tell the Kapo about my hands. Whatever the outcome might be, I had no choice. I went over to him and told him why I had dropped the bag of cement before.

He told the foreman, who looked at me and said: 'All right, then. Leave him alone for now, but don't let me see him here tomorrow. Cripples are no use to me. Tell the camp authorities to pickle him.'

I did nothing for the rest of the day. I sat down on a bag of cement and watched my companions slaving away, to the constant accompaniment of blows and curses. As I sat there, all my experiences went through my mind and I marvelled at having escaped with my life so far. The question was, however, whether my luck would hold out. Only God knew the answer and only He could help me. Father, mother, friends—they could not help me now. Only God, in whose omnipotence I felt an everlasting faith. Looked at with the human eye and weighed up realistically, my situation was hopeless, but I had been in seemingly hopeless situations before and come through them alive.

My thoughts turned to my people, the Jews. The Egyptians had been the first to try and destroy them, but without success. After them had come many others and they, too, had failed. The Nazis would be no more successful than the rest. But in the meantime they were inflicting horrible wounds, which would take a long time to heal.

'His days are numbered,' the other prisoners muttered, and I did not blame them for thinking so, because that was how things looked. But I was not ready to give in yet. I would hope until my dying breath, for I was unshakeably convinced that Providence would not desert me. I had had signs of it from heaven. I remembered what my teacher had told me, my miraculous survival at Bodrog-Keresztur, the wonder rabbi's promises in my dream. All these events I regarded as a sign from heaven that I would survive and that God would continue to watch over me. I would not lose hope, but would raise my eyes to heaven and beg God to have pity on me. He would not forsake me, just as he had not forsaken me up till now.

It was a beautiful day, warm and sunny, a real spring day. If I had not had to sit and watch my comrades suffer, I would have enjoyed my idleness. And the sun was doing my feet good.

A young boy of my own age, streaming with sweat from the effort of carrying the heavy bags of cement, said to me: 'How I envy you. You don't have to slave like me.' He did not know that there was not so much to envy me for.

I told him: 'If you want to envy somebody, envy the people who are a long way from here, in Honolulu or somewhere like that, where the Gestapo can't reach them. Or better still, envy those who have departed this world and no longer have to suffer.' He nodded in agreement.

Another boy, equally unaware of the reason for my inactivity, begged me tearfully to help him hoist another bag of cement onto his shoulders because he no longer had the strength to do it himself. I tried to explain why I could not help him, but he would not believe me, and shook his head, as if to say: 'What a despicable creature, he won't even help a fellow prisoner, but sits around doing

nothing while I am nearly dead from exhaustion.'
I was so chagrined that I started to weep. My tears
convinced him, and when another prisoner told
him that I was the one who had been given the
flogging, I saw that he was sorry he had doubted me.

The rest of the day passed without further incident, and at half-past seven work ended for the
day. We were counted and then marched to the so-
called 'pit-head' where most of the prisoners
worked, and where we all assembled for the march
back to the camp.

The command 'pit-head' was at the foot of a
mountain, which was to be hollowed out into a
bomb-proof aircraft factory. A deep shaft was being
dug into the heart of the mountain.

On the march back to the camp my feet were cut
about still more and I left bloody footprints behind
me at every step. We reached the camp at last and
immediately paraded for roll-call. We had to wait
an hour before the commandant appeared, and
when he arrived he shouted and yelled like a mad-
man. Something must have happened to displease
him, but we did not then know what. Later, we
heard that the camp clerk had got drunk and been
kicked half to death by the commandant. As a
result, he had had to go absent, and now the
camp's accounting had gone awry.

The roll-call ended and we were marched to our block, where our bread ration was distributed. They gave us each a small piece of salami, too, but most of us did not want to eat it because it was supposed to be made with human flesh. Whether this horrible rumour was true or not, the very mention of it turned my stomach, and I threw my piece of salami away.

After this came the lice inspection, which passed off all right for me. Nothing noteworthy happened in the block that night. Two men were flogged because they had dropped a heavy cauldron with our evening soup in it, and another man was kicked by the block senior for coming in with his cap on. At midnight I was at last able to lie down, and fell into an exhausted sleep. Everyone who still had shoes took them with him into his bunk. The block senior said nothing, a sign that he had been responsible for stealing our shoes the night before.

THE THIRD DAY IN MELK

The next day I could not go to where I had been sent to work the day before, because the foreman had forbidden me to show my face there. The Kapo whose group I had been in made sure I was not in his group this time.

The pre-work roll-call was soon over, as usual, since this meant that we could be taken off to work that much earlier. In the evening, of course, the roll-call took much longer, sometimes lasting all night, so that we had to go out to work in the morning without having slept a wink.

Naturally, marching to work did not do my feet any good and they began to grow inflamed and extremely painful. There was a sick bay in the camp, but Jews were never given any treatment there.

I had been assigned to a new place of work, where the prisoners were engaged in digging ditches. Here, too, I was in trouble, because I could not hold my shovel properly. The Kapo stormed over to me. 'What way is that to hold a shovel?' he shouted, getting ready to hit me. The civilian in charge of the work heard him and came over to see what the trouble was. He asked me what was the matter, and it was easy to see from the way he spoke to me that he was not the beating type. I told him that my hands had been frozen and had no strength in them now, which was why I couldn't hold my shovel properly. He looked at me thoughtfully, as if turning over in his mind what to do. Then he shook his head and said: 'What a state your feet are in.'

Taking me by the arm he led me to a small hut where he had his office. His desk was piled high with files. He asked me how old I was, and what had happened to my parents, and then wanted to know all about me. I felt that he was to be trusted and told him the whole story.

'It is an absolute disgrace, what is being done in the name of the German people,' he shouted angrily. 'Our name is being besmirched for ever. Things are reaching such a pass that one is becoming ashamed of being a German! The trouble is that we are forced to stand by helplessly and watch all these atrocities. Anyone who dares to say a word is soon finished off.'

I looked at him unbelievingly, this elderly man of well over sixty. It hardly seemed possible that there could actually be Germans who felt as he did. Until then I had seen only Germans who were cruel and savage. As far as I was concerned, a German was a man who knew how to use a whip and how to hit a prisoner across the head with a rifle butt, or train a machine-gun on him. Yet here in front of me stood a German who was moved to tears by my tale of suffering. Perhaps he was playing with me? No, he could not be. His tears were genuine, they were no crocodile tears. 'Perhaps he isn't a German,' I thought to myself. 'He's certainly not a Chinese or an Indian or a half-caste, though. He must be a German or, as he would probably put it, a pure Aryan.'

He pushed a chair over towards his desk and said: 'If anyone in uniform comes in bend over these plans with me and pretend to be looking at them.' The plans were a mass of lines and curves which meant absolutely nothing to me. 'What if they ask me about them?'

'Don't worry,' replied the superintendent, 'they don't understand the first thing about them.'

In the course of the day, a number of soldiers came into the hut, but seeing me immersed in the plans, took no notice of me. Thus, the whole day passed off safely and peacefully for me. When I say 'peacefully', my meaning is relative, since I could hear the cries of pain from my comrades as they were whipped and beaten all the time.

The superintendent shared his sandwiches with me and even gave me a glass of milk, the first milk

I had even seen for four months. That day was the best in the whole time I had spent in a concentration camp. If only the succeeding days could be as easy, then I would be able to bear everything else.

The time passed all too quickly, and with a heavy heart I prepared to rejoin my fellow prisoners for the march back to camp. The superintendent said that, if I came again the next day, he would treat me the same way. All he asked of me was not to tell anybody about it and not to mention what we had talked about, because it would be dangerous for him. I promised to do as he asked and kept my promise.

The tribulations of the march back soon obliterated the pleasantness of the day. Even though my comrades helped me as much as they could, I could barely walk. Every time I put a foot to the ground it felt as if someone were jabbing a dagger into it. Although there were plenty of doctors among the prisoners, they had no bandages or ointment and no medicine, so there was not much they could do for me. There were not even any rags anywhere for me to tie round my feet. I thought of tearing a piece off my striped prison shirt, but that was Reich property and to tear it was considered sabotage, which was punishable by death. If I had still had shoes I might have risked it, because they would have hidden anything I might have wrapped round my feet. But I had no shoes.

I was very worried as I lay down on my bunk that night, because I did not know what would happen the next day when I tried to march out to work. Anybody who could not keep up with his group was helped along with a gun butt, and the blows rained down on him until he either reached his work-place or fell dead. But worrying would not help me. There was nobody I could turn to in the camp, so the only thing to do was to look to heaven for help. Only God could save me. I prayed in silence, for He understands our prayers, even when we do not move our lips. He can read the language of our hearts. And, praying, I fell asleep.

THE FOURTH DAY
IN MELK

At the first sound of the morning whistle I jumped out of my bunk and looked for someone to help me arrange it properly, not a difficult task, since my fellow prisoners were always ready to give whatever help they could when it was needed.

On this, my fourth day in Melk, instead of going out to work, twenty prisoners would be staying behind in the camp to clean it up, and I was fortunate enough to be one of them. Thank God, I thought to myself, thank God. He had heard my prayer of the day before and answered it. My main worry had been the march to work since, once there, the civilian superintendent would have looked after me all right. However, with my feet in the condition they were in, I could never have endured the march.

The job for today could be accounted an easy one and it was, moreover, not so strictly supervised since, unlike the other jobs, it was of no importance to the war effort.

The foreman in charge was a Jewish prisoner, and he let me sit down and do nothing all day, out of

135

pity. But my feet troubled me very much and steadily grew even more painful. They were running with pus, and everyone felt sorry for me. Sympathy was all they had to offer, but it did not help to ease my pain. I felt wretched and desolate. If there is really a hell, it could not be worse than this, I thought to myself. Why did my life have to be saved? Why had I not been killed by that Nazi's bullets at Bodrog-Keresztur? Why had I been saved by a miracle, when my ward-mate had torn the poisoned chocolate out of the nurse's hands? What had impelled me to leave the hospital? All these and many other questions I asked myself, thinking that it would have been better to have died in the gas-chambers of Auschwitz than to suffer as I was suffering now.

I was no longer so certain that all my miraculous escapes were due to God's pity. Perhaps they were just the opposite. Perhaps I was being kept alive so that I could be punished still more. After all, was I better than those to whom no miracles had happened?

Enough, I decided. I must stop thinking like that, for if I did not, there would be a danger that I would start having doubts about my faith. I had lost everything—family, freedom, health, and my faith in God was all I had left. If I kept allowing my earlier thoughts to come untrammelled, I might lose the last possession I still had, the one that was most holy of all, my faith.

My head fell forward, my eyes closed and I fell into a deep sleep.

I felt someone shaking my arm, and when I opened my eyes my heart missed a beat. Standing in front of me were the camp commandant and his tall bodyguard. I was sure my last moment had come.

'What's going on here? What is the matter with this boy?' demanded the commandant.

The man in charge, scared to death and as white as a sheet, could not speak a word.

'Why doesn't somebody see that his feet are bandaged?' the commandant barked. 'Tell the Kapo to come here.'

The camp resounded with shouts of 'Camp Kapo, camp Kapo, report to the commandant, report to the commandant!'

The Kapo was there in a flash, clicking his heels and awaiting orders. 'This boy's feet must be bandaged immediately. Understood?'

'Yes, sir. Right away, sir.'

The commandant turned away from me, and I heard him say to his adjutant: 'He can hardly be more than ten years old. I feel sorry for children.'

Meanwhile, the Kapo had lost no time in running

to the sick-bay and coming back with a doctor. He took one look at my feet and said that I would have to come to the sick-bay and have them cleaned up before they could be bandaged. The camp Kapo, the most feared of all his colleagues, put me across his shoulder and took me to the sick-bay himself.

The doctor cleaned my feet, wiped them over with an antiseptic, put a paper bandage on them. Then he even gave me a sedative, since the commandant had ordered that I must be looked after. The Kapo took me back to my hut, telling me to stay there and rest, and the block senior allowed me to lie on my bunk, something normally unthinkable during the daytime.

My feet were much less painful now. As I lay on my bunk, thoughts started crowding into my brain again. Had all that had just happened been yet another miracle? All my fellow prisoners would say it had been. And if it had been, was it the last or would there be more, enough to bring me safely out of this living hell? My courage began to return. I would survive, I told myself. I must survive!

THE FIFTH DAY IN MELK

The day started badly for me. The moment I got out of my bunk, a heavy blow on the back sent me sprawling. I had no idea why I had been hit, because I had got up at the first sound of the whistle, but I had no desire to turn round and see who had hit me. What was the point? In any case, it was far more important to move out of the way before the next blow descended. I just managed to do so, and made my way outside to go to the latrines. It was pouring with rain and I was soaked to the skin in seconds, my prison clothes, made of some synthetic material, clinging wetly to me. At least I would not have to wash this morning. The paper bandage on my feet disintegrated and floated away. 'God giveth and God taketh away,' I thought to myself as the rain lashed down. To crown everything, I had lost my belt, a grievous loss, since my trousers were far too big for me and would not stay up without something to hold them.

I did not want to accuse anyone of having stolen the belt. I might well have lost it. Either way, however, the fact remained that I had nothing to keep my trousers up with.

I joined the long queue for the latrines. The

excrement chief grinned and gave me a powerful kick. To him I was a freak, something one saw at a side-show, and I was fair game for his little jokes, which usually took the form of a push, a blow or, as now, a hard kick.

However, I was far more worried about my feet. I turned over in my mind whether or not to go to the sick-bay. After all, they had been so solicitous there yesterday, after the commandant had said that my feet must be bandaged. But it was a long way to go in the pouring rain, and I did not think I could make it unaided. Just then I looked up and saw Levy, my old schoolmate. I knew he would do me a favour if I asked him and, sure enough, when I said I wanted to go to the sick-bay, he came with me and helped me along. I could hardly expect him to carry me over his shoulder. He had always been a weakling and camp life would hardly have helped to build him up.

When we were only a short distance from the sick-bay, he told me to go on alone and that he would wait for me and take me back to my hut after treatment. A guard stood in front of the sick bay, not a soldier, but a prisoner. I went up to him and asked him to let me in. He looked at me with contempt and yelled at me: 'Get away from here, you ragged creature!'

As I turned away to go back to my waiting friend, I trod on the bottom of one of my trousers legs, and before I could recover my balance had fallen flat on my face in the mud. Laboriously, I picked myself up and joined my waiting friend. He had seen everything, and tried to console me by saying that bandaging my feet would not have helped much, since the paper bandage would have disintegrated the moment I had put a foot outside the sick-bay door.

He was right, of course, but what a pity he had not thought of it earlier and saved us a long, weary trudge. Come to that, I should have thought of it myself, but my brain did not seem to be working as well as it once had. This was hardly to be wondered at in the circumstances.

By the time I got back to the hut, all the coffee was gone. I had needed it today more than ever.

Today, Dr Hirsch, a thin, fair-haired man, had been appointed block doctor, although nobody yet knew what his duties would consist of, since there were no bandages or drugs for him. Nevertheless he had been told not to go out to work with the other prisoners any more.

He was next to me as we went to fall in for the roll-call, in the usual five rows, and offered to carry me to the parade-ground on his shoulders. He was by no means certain that the block senior would agree to this, so he did not ask him, hoping that he would not see from his position at the head of the group. Luck was with us, and we arrived safely at the parade-ground. But after the roll-call, Dr Hirsch would go back to the hut and I would have to go out to work, so he asked the prisoners standing on either side of me to hold me up during the march to work, and they promised to do so.

That morning the roll-call lasted more than an hour. The commandant had probably overslept. I looked at my feet and blenched. It really was a miracle that I had not contracted blood poisoning. As I was looking down, I heard a prisoner say to his companion: 'He is a candidate, all right.' In camp slang, this meant, 'a candidate for death'. But death, even when one longed for it, because it solved everything, was not easy to achieve, even here.

How often in this place, one heard prisoners expressing envy of another prisoner who had had his wish granted and had died. How often in this place one heard men saying that all they wished was to die in peace. It did not matter where: in the woods, in a field, anywhere, as long as they could breathe their last in peace. But not here, because here they marched you and worked you for as long as you could draw breath. If you said your feet could not take you a step further, they helped you along with whips. You were whipped until even they could see that you could not go on because your lungs could no longer draw in the air you needed to live. Then they believed you and did not force you to go out to work. But they did not leave you in peace. First came the dentist, who took a forceps out of his pocket and prised your mouth open. If he saw any gold fillings, or indeed fillings of any precious metal, he would knock the teeth out of your mouth with a special little hammer. He was followed by the camp clerk, who wanted to make sure that the number he had been given was identical with the one tattooed on your arm. After him came the corpse bearers, who picked you up, threw you onto a stretcher and took you to the cellar under the headquarters building. There they dumped you, like a sack of potatoes, onto the pile of other 'liberated prisoners'. Your card was taken out of the file in the camp office for the last time and marked, 'Dead'. But no doctor wrote the cause of death on your card. The clerk had a whole list of causes of death in his drawer. He chose any one he fancied and wrote it on your card.

Your corpse stayed where it had been thrown until the following Saturday. The camp crematorium was still under construction, so the bodies had to be taken to the Mauthausen concentration camp to be burnt. Every Saturday, a big lorry was loaded high with corpses and sent off to Mauthausen.

The whole ghastly sequence passed before my mind's eye. That would be my fate unless another miracle happened, a miracle like the one that time when a big, black dog had been sent to tear me to pieces and had come and licked my face instead.

The roll-call came to an end. Soon the march to work would begin. I looked round the group I was in and saw young Weiss, with whom I had studied in Nagykaroly. I asked him to come and stand next to me, so that he could help me when the double marching started. I could see from his face that this would not be easy for him, because he was near the end of his tether himself. But he could not bring himself to refuse, especially when he saw that I was in an even worse state than he was. He came over straightaway and gave me his arm. By the time we came to where the cattle-trucks were waiting, my feet were almost torn to ribbons. The journey was agony. The trucks were crammed so full that people were standing all over my feet. My screams of agony did not help, because we were packed together so tightly that they could not possibly move away.

By the time we arrived at our destination, I looked

as if I had just come out of a Turkish bath. My luck still held, however, and I was again sent to the building site I had been sent to two days earlier, where the superintendent had allowed me to sit in his office and share his sandwiches.

As soon as he saw me, he came over. He looked at me for a few moments without saying anything, and tears sprang into his eyes. Then he took my arm and led me into his hut. As soon as we were inside the door he said: 'Who is responsible for your being in such a condition? You look frightful.' He took a few quick steps away from me, brought an armful of sticks and lit the stove. Then he removed my drenched clothing and hung it over a line to dry, giving me his raincoat to put on.

Just as he had done two days before, he let me sit at his desk and spread a drawing out in front of me. If anyone should come in, I was to pretend, as before, to be poring over it.

At about ten o'clock he offered me a ham sandwich, but I refused it, telling him that my religion forbade it. 'I am surprised that you are so true to your religion. You are in such a bad way that I am sure that God would forgive you if you were not to be quite so observant.'

'You are right,' I told him, 'my religion allows exceptions in cases of dire need. It is in fact a duty to eat what is normally forbidden if starvation is the only alternative. However, as I have never eaten any pig meat in my life, I don't think I could swallow it.'

'That's different,' he said and dropped the subject. He took the ham himself and left me the bread. Then he took a small bottle out of a drawer and poured me a glass of spirits. 'My own make,' he said. 'I know something about blending spirits because my father used to own a distillery and entrusted me with all his trade secrets when I was still only a lad. When my father died, I sold the business, because I couldn't stand the smell of brandy any more.'

He asked me what I had studied, and since I trusted him completely I told him that I had been a student in a rabbinical seminary. He was pleased about that and said that he knew the Bible well and still read it in his free time. He had often stayed with his uncle, who was a bishop, he told me. He had learnt a great deal about the Bible from his uncle, and had often had discussions with Jewish scholars before the war, but now this was, of course, impossible. The more so, he added, since the authorities were suspicious of anybody who was interested in that kind of thing. However, now was a good chance, and he would be grateful if I could explain various matters that particularly interested him. Of course, I told him, I was far from having a complete knowledge of the subject, but I would answer all his questions as far as I was able.

Why did the Bible forbid Jews to eat pig meat, he wanted to know. He had been given one explanation but he had not found it convincing.

'What was the explanation you heard?' I asked.

'Because the climate in Palestine is very hot and pig meat is so fatty that it is inimical to one's health.'

'Why didn't this explanation satisfy you?'

'Because you are also forbidden to eat the flesh of various other animals which aren't at all fatty or greasy.'

'All our religious sages have rejected that explanation, too, on the same grounds as yourself. The correct one is that everything a man eats has some influence on his soul and character. If, for example, a man lived on animals of prey, he or his descendants would in time assume some of those animals' characteristics and develop a certain inclination towards cruelty. Actually, all the animals whose flesh we are forbidden to eat are animals of prey or scavengers. The pig certainly is.'

'That answer satisfies me,' the superintendent declared, shaking me by the hand.

Next, he wanted to know why Jews slaughtered

animals for food by cutting their throats, a method of slaughter Nazi propaganda described as primitive, barbaric and cruel. I explained that bleeding to death was the most painless method of dying. When an animal had its throat cut, it lost consciousness immediately and bled to death without feeling the slightest pain. 'Yes,' he said, 'I can vouch for the truth of that. I was badly wounded during the First World War and lost so much blood that I became unconscious, but I didn't feel any pain.'

When my clothes were dry, the superintendent looked them over and stiched up any small tears he found. He even sewed on two missing buttons, and then handed me the clothes so that I could get dressed. He apologized for not being able to give me any shoes. Regulations strictly forbade even the smallest item of clothing or anything else being given to prisoners, and it had been known for soldiers to be sent to a concentration camp for giving a prisoner something. Moreover, he was always inspected by the troops on guard duty when he came to the site. However, he did give me his belt to keep my trousers up.

Many of the troops on guard duty did not share the viewpoint of the Nazis, he told me, but were forced to keep silent because one word out of place might well cost them their lives.

148

We could hear the cries of prisoners as the Kapo began hitting them, and the superintendent exclaimed: 'There he goes again, the swine. I can't do anything about it because I have received the strictest instructions not to interfere. In fact, they have even given me a whip and told me to flog any prisoner not pulling his weight, but I have never used it and never will.'

He took the whip out of a drawer and showed it to me. 'Here it is. I'll keep it as a souvenir.'

When the Kapo dished out the soup at midday, he gave me a double portion because he had noticed that I had become the superintendent's protégé.

Other prisoners also received an extra portion of soup, but only on condition that they paid for it by bending over and receiving a lash of his whip. Whether the soup was sufficiently nourishing to make this worth while, I did not know. The doctors among us used to have long discussions as to whether the whiplash did more to weaken a man than the extra portion of soup strengthened him.

The guards found the scene so amusing that they were helpless with laughter, going into fresh paroxysms every time an unfortunate prisoner received the whip across his back for the extra soup he was getting.

When I had finished my soup, I went back to the

superintendent's hut and spent the whole afternoon there in peace. Before I left for the march back, I again had to promise to keep the day's happenings to myself and not divulge what we had talked about.

The Kapo, seeing that the superintendent had a soft spot for me, himself treated me somewhat better that evening. He told two prisoners to help me during the march back to camp. Once there, we paraded for the evening roll-call, which dragged on and on, with endless countings and re-countings that went on until three in the morning. At first, we all wondered what had happened, but the news soon spread among the prisoners: a Russian officer had escaped, and the camp authorities wanted to find out which one it was.

As each prisoner's number was called, he had to shout, 'Here', but this, of course, was no check since somebody shouted 'Here' for every number that was called. The S.S. men were furious. Somebody was definitely missing because they had counted us and found one short, but they soon had the idea of making each prisoner step forward when his number was called. All they had to do then was to see that the number on the list and the number tattooed on the prisoner's arm tallied. Eventually they found out who the missing prisoner was.

The exciting thought that at least one of us had

managed to escape made the interminable roll-call bearable, especially as the S.S. men were so obviously discomfited because someone might manage to evade their clutches.

Fortunately, the next day was a Sunday, and we would not have to go out to work, so the fact that the roll-call lasted so long was not as disastrous as it might have been. If the next day had been a working day, we would have had to go out to work without any sleep at all. Not that we had every Sunday off. Oh no, that would have made life too easy! Every alternate Sunday was the rule, and we were fortunate that our work-free Sunday happened to be the next day and not the following week.

The roll-call ended at last and we went back to our huts. The block senior made an exception and cancelled the lice inspection, so we were given our bread ration and fell onto our bunks, but not before two prisoners had been flogged for not having made up their bunks in the morning in the manner prescribed by regulations.

BAD NEWS DAY

Our free Sundays were always called 'bad news days', because we were allowed to visit relatives and friends in the other parts of the camp, and there was always bad news for someone. Sons discovered that their fathers had been killed, uncles that their nephews were dead, brothers that they were now alone in the world.

My feet were too painful for me to do any visiting, even though I had many friends in the camp whom I would have liked to see. I just lay on my bunk all day, and when the time for the evening roll-call came, Dr Hirsch carried me to the parade-ground on his shoulders. After it was over, and he had carried me back, I had a visitor I was very glad to see. He came from my home town and had been my best friend at school.

But the evening was to end sadly. After we had talked for hours about 'the good old times', he suddenly became **very** grave. Taking his bread ration from his trousers pocket he held it out towards me.

'I can't take your bread ration!' I exclaimed.

'Take it, I don't need bread any more.'

'What are you talking about?'

'I shall die tonight, that's why I don't need any bread.'

'Have you gone out of your mind? You have always been deeply religious and you know very well that suicide is a sin.'

'Suicide is a sin when any possibility of life still remains, but it is permitted when there is no longer any such possibility. I cannot see any possibility of anything that could be called life, here.'

I used all my powers of persuasion to try and make him change his mind. I quoted the Talmud to him, argued with him, cajoled him, upbraided him—all to no avail. It had to be done and it had to be done that night, he said. And nothing could move him from his resolve. Finally, I had exhausted all my arguments and fell silent. He wanted to give me his shoes as well, but I refused to accept them.

Before he left me, he asked me to keep his secret. 'If you should survive the war and see my parents, don't tell them how I met my end,' he begged me. I promised, thinking to myself that he would not go through with it. He kissed me on the forehead and said: 'You will come through all right because you have courage.' Then he was gone.

THE SEVENTH DAY
IN MELK

When the whistle woke me next morning, I realized that I had slept in my prison clothes, a breach of the regulations that would have earned me a flogging if I had been caught. Fortunately, nobody in authority noticed.

I crawled to the latrines on all fours. They were a-buzz with talk of a young boy who had run as hard as he could towards the barbed wire fence and had been shot by the guards. Everyone was speculating as to who it could have been. I was probably the only person who knew, but I kept quiet.

So he had gone through with it. I said a prayer, because he had asked me the evening before to remember him in my prayers. All round me the prisoners were saying: 'He is out of it now. The S.S. can't hurt him any more.'

It was almost time for the morning roll-call. Dr Hirsch carried me there once more and saw to it that two of my companions would help me along on the march to work. Once there, I would be all right, because the superintendent would let me sit in his hut and not make me work.

But it was not to be. One of the Kapos needed a hundred prisoners for his group, but as fast as he rounded them up they sidled away and joined other groups. The other Kapos came to the aid of their colleague, forcing prisoners to join the group to make the number up. Before I knew what had happened I had been pushed into the group as well.

I did not know why everyone was so anxious not to be in this particular group, but I was soon to find out. We marched a quarter of a mile or so further, and then we reached the place where we were to work. The overseer here was a non-com., but not a member of the S.S.

Some railway wagons loaded with stones stood nearby, and he ordered us to split up into pairs, one pair to each railway wagon. Our job was to unload them, and he gave us fifteen minutes to do it in.

My work-mate was a youth of my own age. He jumped up onto a wagon and picked up a shovel. I did not even have the strength to climb up onto the wagon unaided, so he gave me his hand and pulled me up. When I tried to pick up a shovel, it fell from my hands. My companion said nothing. He could see that I was in no fit state to work at all, so he just set to and tried to do enough work for both of us. It was an impossible task. It would have taken two strong, healthy men more than an hour to unload the wagon, and we had been given fifteen minutes. Not only could I not help, but I was in agony from the sharp stones which were digging into my feet.

The short, fat overseer looked at his wrist-watch, counting the seconds like a time-keeper at a boxing match. He was obviously pleased that nobody emptied a wagon in the time he had set them. Now he could take revenge on these lazy, work-shy enemies of the mighty German Reich.

No wonder everyone had tried to join some other work party.

He was not much under sixty, this non-commissioned officer of the Wehrmacht, the German armed forces. Although not a member of the S.S., he did not lag behind them in his devotion to duty. That day he had devised a new form of punishment. Climbing up onto a pile of unloaded stones he began hurling them at his lazy work-team, who had been unable to finish emptying the wagons in the set time of fifteen minutes. Everyone began to duck out of the way of the flying, fist-sized stones, but I was not nimble enough and one hit me full on the side of the head, knocking me out. When I came to, I was lying face downward on the stones, my head covered in blood—and somebody in hob-nailed boots was stamping on my body, shouting: 'Enough,

enough! Get up!' I was seized by a tremendous rage and, not caring any more what might happen, I shouted back at the overseer, for they were his boots that were pounding me: 'Go on, you murderer, kick me to death! You savage animal, you!' To my amazement, he stopped kicking me.

'I'll kill you when I want to, not when you want me to,' he growled and stamped off to beat and kick some other poor unfortunate.

I fainted again, regaining consciousness in time to feel myself being bundled off a stretcher like a sack of potatoes. I looked around me and saw that I had been brought to the cellars where the corpses were dumped to await collection by the truck at the week-end. The stretcher-bearers looked at me in horror and amazement. They had thought I was dead, they told me, when they had recovered from their shock. I had been booked out as dead, and they had been told to throw my body in with the other bodies.

Something felt wrong with my mouth, but I could not for the moment make out what it was. Then I realized. The one gold-filled tooth I had had was missing. The dentist had knocked it out with his little hammer.

The two prisoners who had brought me to the cellar did not know what to do now. I was stark naked, having been stripped when I was booked out as dead, according to regulations, and was shivering with cold. 'Take me back to my hut,' I begged them, and they finally agreed. They lifted me back onto the stretcher, put me on the floor of my hut, and went off to their own hut in another part of the camp.

The block senior was busy with the lice inspection and had no time to pay any attention to me. Nor was my nakedness in any way unusual, because everyone had to strip for the inspection.

When he had finished examining all the prisoners, the block senior turned to me. 'What are you doing here. You've already been booked out as dead! Have you risen from the dead like Jesus Christ?' I told him what had happened, but he did not want to hear. 'I can't take you back in this block. No, it's impossible. You'll have to go back to the cellars. Even if you are still alive today, you're bound to be dead by tomorrow or the day after. I haven't got any food for you in any case, and your bunk is occupied.' He called to two prisoners to take me back to the cellars.

My comrades had gathered round me, and they begged the block senior to help me.

'How can I help him? He has been booked out as dead and his file closed.'

'Still, Mr Block Senior, do something for him.'

He thought it over and then relented. 'All right, he can stay here for tonight. We'll try and get him put back on the camp books, but I can't promise that it'll work. I've got no food for him. All he can have is some coffee. There is enough of that.' He pointed to a corner where I was allowed to lie down on the stone floor. There were no blankets for me, so I had to lie down naked, but when the lights were put out somebody threw me one. He had obviously waited until then so that the block senior would not see what he was doing.

I fell asleep, wondering why I had had to recover consciousness instead of just dying where I had been thrown, and what would happen to me in the morning.

My fellow-prisoners and I had been the first Jewish prisoners to be sent to Melk. One of the camp buildings, formerly an army sick-bay, was barred to Jews at first, and was given a very wide berth by all the other prisoners. All sorts of sinister things went on in the sick-bay. People who were admitted with comparatively harmless diseases used to die mysteriously. Also, a big closed lorry used to call there from time to time, take on a load of patients, and drive off. Nobody knew where they were taken to, but one thing was certain: nobody ever saw them alive again.

As the light came on, I heard the block doctor shouting: 'An important order from the commandant! No sick prisoner is to parade for morning roll-call. Anyone who feels ill must report immediately to the sick-bay.' I did not know whether this applied to me as well, because no decision had been taken yet as to whether I belonged with the living prisoners or the dead ones, so I lay where I was.

'Where is the boy I always have to carry on my shoulders? Why doesn't he report?' shouted the doctor. I crawled towards him on all fours, and as he caught sight of me, he yelled: 'Do you think I am always going to carry you on my shoulders? Why don't you report sick immediately? Are you waiting for them to send a special messenger for you? Why are you naked? Where are your clothes?' Without waiting for my answers, he lifted me onto his shoulders and took me over to the sick-bay, where the entrance was crowded with prisoners.

Only the most serious cases would be taken in, we were told, and the S.S. doctor in charge picked them out. 'This one can stay,' he said when he saw me. Dr Hirsch took me inside. I was given a shirt and put into a small room where there were already four patients.

All there was in the room was five wooden bunks, each with a sack full of shavings serving as a mattress. There were no sheets, no nurses and no toilet facilities of any kind for those too ill to get out of bed.

That same night Dr Hirsch was appointed 'sick-bay doctor'. He was a decent person and helped in any way he could.

Prisoners in the sick-bay did not have to attend roll-calls, but were counted in their beds twice a day by S.S. men. That morning, however, the figures did not tally apparently, for people kept bursting in and counting us again. This went on for two hours, and then, at eight o'clock, the block clerk and another man rushed in, seized hold of me and carried me down to the cellar again. I asked why I was being taken there and was told: 'You were wrongly entered in the books.'

As I lay there among a pile of corpses, an S.S. man came in and counted them, including me in the total. Even though he could see that I was alive he showed no interest in me whatever.

This was Wednesday. I prayed to God that I would die before Saturday, when the lorry came to take away the corpses for burning in the Mauthausen crematoria. I did not want to be burned alive.

On the cellar wall, someone had daubed in blood:

'Comrades, when the time comes, and it certainly will come, take your revenge on this barbaric, bloodthirsty nation.' A Russian had written it, dipping his finger into his own blood. He had jumped out of a moving train to try and escape, and a wheel had gone over his leg. The Nazis threw him into the cellar, where he lingered on in agony for a few days, calling for water the whole time. But everybody was strictly forbidden to give him any, or any food either.

Now and again I said a prayer for the dead lying all round me. There were thirty-seven of them. I knew, because I had heard the S.S. man count them.

I lay there thinking of death and heaven, where I would be reunited with my family. How long would it take my soul to get there? At school, I had learnt that the distance to the stars was measured in light-years and that there were some stars which were thousands, even millions of years away. A man's soul would have to move at a fantastic speed to reach heaven at all. Then I remembered my grandfather saying: 'Distance exists only for material things. Since the soul is not a material thing, it is in heaven the moment it is released from the body, and there is no such concept as distance in heaven.'

Towards evening, the cellar door opened and the clerk appeared. 'You can come back to the sick-bay now,' he said. He explained that, in the morning, the count had not tallied because the S.S. had found one prisoner too many alive and one corpse too few. Only after some time had they realized that I had been wrongly entered in the books. I owed it to him that I had been transferred to the living total, the clerk said, hoisting me onto his shoulders and taking me back to my room.

The bread ration had already been distributed, but there was some soup left over from midday, so I was given some of that.

I looked round the room at my fellow-patients. The one next to me was a Pole, a Kapo known as 'the fireman'. Not because it was his job to put out fires, but because he loved to punish prisoners who had done something wrong by making them strip and drenching them with ice-cold water from a hose until they died. He must have killed literally hundreds this way. I had no need to fear him now, since a Kapo lost his title when he fell ill and only regained it when he got better. And unless a miracle happened, the Pole was not going to get better, my room-mates said. A broad red streak ran from his knee right up to his heart, a symptom of blood poisoning. The Pole told us that it was all a prisoner's fault. He had fallen while flogging a prisoner, and broken his knee. 'When I get better, the swine will have nothing to laugh about,' threatened the Pole. But he would not be able to exact the vengeance he thirsted for, because his condition was worsening from hour to hour.

I cannot say that I felt any sympathy for him. On the contrary, I felt a certain satisfaction that here, where evil was king, a spark of justice was discernible. Nevertheless, I could not bring myself to refuse to give him water when he groaned and begged for it. My companions did not view my action very favourably, but I remembered a saying from the Talmud: 'Do not throw stones at him who has fallen,' and this impelled me to help the man.

After two days he fell into a delirium from which he never regained consciousness. His last words were 'I'll flay you all to ribbons, you swine!' When he was dead, two Kapos came and stood by his bunk to pay their respects. After a quarter of an hour, they saluted, picked up his corpse and hurled it into the cellars. There were supplies of drugs and medicines in the sick-bay, but their use to treat Jews was strictly forbidden. Furthermore, anybody suffering from pneumonia, heart disease or similar illnesses was refused admission.

Twice a week, my feet were smeared with some kind of black ointment, but instead of making them better, it made them worse. However, I did not worry overmuch about this since, once my feet were cured, I would have to leave the sick-bay and go back to the hut and outside working-parties.

We were given the same rations as the other camp inmates. I had a big appetite and, after a few days, I found a way of augmenting them. There was always an appreciable quantity of soup left in the cauldron after everybody had received his ration, and after the distribution was over, the cauldron was left in the wash-room, to which we had access, until the evening, when it was taken back to the kitchen and filled with coffee, ready for our evening meal of bread and coffee. The S.S. man in charge was always absent during the early afternoon, and the sick-bay Kapo and his clerk used to go back to their rooms after their meal for a rest, so it was then that I always made my way to the wash-room and finished off whatever soup was left at the bottom of the cauldron.

Gradually, I began to recover from my earlier privations, and my companions started commenting on how well I was looking. I was regaining the use of my hands, too, though they were still far from being strong enough for me to do any work with them.

After two weeks, all my room-mates were moved out and their places were taken by others. One of those who had been sent back to work was so badly beaten, three or four days afterwards, that he was re-admitted and died the same night.

Once, when I had to go the latrine, I did not want to have to put my naked, injured feet on the stinking, urine-soaked patch of floor immediately in front of the urinal, so I stood further back from it than usual in order to relieve myself. As bad luck would have it, the block clerk came in at that moment, saw me and thought that I was going to urinate on the floor. He began to hit me, and as he did so, who should come in but the S.S. man. 'He was urinating on the floor,' the block clerk said.

'Bend over,' the S.S. man told me, curtly. I did so, waiting for the usual twenty-five strokes. But after he had dealt me two murderous blows with the thick truncheon he always carried, the S.S. man said: 'Well, do you want any more?'

'No thank you,' I replied.

'Well, beat it,' he said. I 'beat it' as quickly as I could.

When I got back to the ward, my fellow-inmates were as much at a loss as I was to understand why I had not received the regulation twenty-five strokes, because it was so out of character for an S.S. man not to mete out punishment when he had the opportunity. The next day, the mystery was solved. The block clerk saw me and said: 'You were lucky yesterday. The S.S. man could not wait any longer, that's why he only had time to give you two whacks. He told me so himself.' I must say, at this point, that the block clerk was not a bully. He will appear in this narrative again, when he shows his more humane side. The only time he hit me was in the urinal, and I have long since forgiven him for that.

Although the S.S. man was called 'Doctor' by all the prisoners, including the doctors among them, it was an open secret that he had no doctor's degree and had not even studied medicine. However, he had grown so used to being called 'Doctor' that he had begun to believe he really was one. One day, his jack-boots started rubbing, and soon his feet were painfully sore. He would not allow himself to be treated by any of the doctors among the prisoners, but treated himself while they all looked on. They could see that he was doing it all wrong, but did not dare to say anything. By the time he had brought himself to consult one of the prisoners, it was already too late. Blood-poisoning had set in. The doctor knew that the S.S. man would now inevitably die, but did not tell him so, and was afraid to treat him in case he would be held responsible for the S.S. man's death, so he advised him to report to a hospital for treatment.

This particular S.S. man had a murderous reputation. Up to 1944 it had been the custom in concentration camps to administer lethal injections to all prisoners unable to work for more than fourteen days because of illness or injuries. He had carried out this task at various concentration camps.

His successor was, happily, much better. Although he was an S.S. man, he did not seem to be a bad fellow. The war was not going so well for Germany by that time, and he could see which way the wind was blowing. In such circumstances, he must have decided that it was better to exercise restraint. Not that he did anything to make our situation any better, but at least he did not beat prisoners unmercifully or kill them. That he hit one occasionally was not so unexpected for an S.S. man. Of course, he might well have committed atrocities at other camps, but I never heard about them.

AIR RAIDS

Every day, Allied aircraft flew overhead in mass formation, apparently without any fear of retaliation, because they carried out their sorties in broad daylight. We could already recognize them as Allied from the note of their engines.

Their appearance kindled new hope in our breasts, for we now felt that we were no longer forgotten and that someone was fighting for us. Nobody could possibly have imagined that we were their target, since our friends were well-informed and knew what kind of people were confined in the camps.

None of us knew exactly what month it was, let alone what day of the week, but on this particular occasion I knew that it was Saturday and that it must be somewhere at the beginning of July. I was lying on my bunk listening to the sound of the aircraft engines, when I realized that, this time, it was going on for far too long. Somebody in a neighbouring bunk suggested that the Allied aircraft were circling overhead in order to encourage us, as if to say: 'Don't be afraid, we are soon coming to set you free.'

The noise of the propellers sounded so sweetly in

my ears that it lulled me to sleep. I awoke to the sound of tremendous explosions, with the ground trembling beneath me. I forced myself to open my eyes, but could hardly see anything through the clouds of thick smoke all round me. I was lying on the floor, my bunk submerged in a mass of splintered wood. One wall of the room was no longer there, and just beyond where it had been was a bomb crater. The bomb had fallen about five feet from where I had been lying.

At first, I could not understand what had happened and thought that the Germans were trying to wipe us out. I turned to see how my companions had fared. What a horrible sight! One of them had been decapitated, his severed head lying some distance from his body. Another had been crushed to death. I could not bear to look any more. Then I thought of examining myself and to my great relief realized that I had not even been scratched.

Outside, the compound was crowded with dead and injured. A thick column of black smoke was rising towards the sky from a burning barrack block. Hands, feet and heads were festooned on the barbed wire, and cries for help could be heard from all directions. I ran from one injured man to another, but soon came to the sad conclusion that there was nothing I could do for any of them, since I had not the slightest knowledge of first aid. Actually, even those among the prisoners who were doctors could not do much for the injured, because they had no bandages or dressings of any kind.

'Write down my name,' begged a badly injured man lying not far from where I was standing. 'If you survive, tell my family what day I died.' There was no paper or pencil in the concentration camp, so he asked if he could dip his finger in his own blood and scrawl his name on my body with it. Although I knew that I would have to wash it off in the end, I granted his request so that he could die with a quiet mind.

Several watch-towers had collapsed, and a number of guards had been killed or wounded. It was this that convinced us that it was the Allies, and not the Germans, who had bombed the camp.

The kitchen had received a direct hit, so no food could be distributed, but who felt hungry?

The much feared chief Kapo (camp policeman) had been killed in the raid. Nobody mourned him then. It was only when his successor turned out to be a thousand times worse that we ceased to feel joyful at his death.

All the badly injured were picked up, loaded onto lorries and taken away that day. They were never seen again.

I hurried back to the hospital barracks, from which my dead companions had already been removed. I lay alone in the room now, with its missing fourth wall. Since nothing more than splinters remained of the bunks, I lay down on the floor. I had stopped going to the sick-bay to have my feet treated, but despite this, my injuries were now beginning to heal very quickly—far too quickly for my liking. Soon they were so much better that I feared I would shortly be discharged from the hospital barracks. That would be a major misfortune. I went back to the sick-bay for some more of the black ointment that had proved so harmful earlier, but alas, even this failed to retard the healing of my legs.

What a topsy-turvy world it had become! Instead of being happy at getting better, one hoped to remain unwell as long as possible. Prisoners used to wish each other 'a good illness'.

TWENTIETH OF JULY

'Nobody goes to work today.' The announcement took us by surprise. What had happened? No one could supply the answer. Then we noticed that there was not a single soldier to be seen anywhere in the camp. Soon, the news had spread like wildfire—there had been an attempt on Hitler's life. Nobody knew where the news had come from. Although there were neither newspapers nor radio in the camp and soldiers were strictly forbidden to talk to prisoners, news got through to us somehow.

That day should have been a selection day, but there was no selection. Prisoners stood around the camp square in groups, not yet daring to show their jubilation openly, but with hearts filled with hope.

The Kapos had laid aside their whips. They did not care about the prisoners or discipline now, but walked up and down with lowered heads. We could see from their faces that they were hoping desperately that the attempt to kill Hitler had failed, for his end would mean theirs also.

We talked about what we would do and where we would go when the camp gates were finally thrown open and we were told: 'You can go! You are free!' I heard one man say that the first thing he would do would be to sit down and eat until he could eat no more. His companion thought it more important first to beat up the camp commandant and then hang him. 'Hang him!' interjected a third. 'That would be too good for him. He should be cut to pieces and salt rubbed into his wounds. The same goes for the Kapos and the block seniors, especially the senior of Block 5, the murderer, and all who have tortured and slaughtered us!'

The soldiers in the watch-towers were uneasy, continually calling out to ask if there was any further news. The soldier in charge of the kitchen had not appeared, so the prisoners who worked there were handing out food to anyone who wanted it. And who did not want it?

The bloodthirsty, much-feared Kapo in charge of the shoe store stood idly by while prisoners broke into it and looted the boots and shoes there, not daring to try and stop anyone. He had turned from a ravening wolf into a mild and gentle sheep. The door of the clothing store was also broken down, and anyone who wished to do so helped himself. In short, there was no supervision anywhere in the camp. Nevertheless, from the watch-towers the muzzles of the machine-guns were still trained menacingly on us and the great gates of the camp remained barred and bolted. Soon, even these last obstacles would be overcome, when . . .

Towards noon, many of the prisoners began to give open expression to their growing feeling of jubilation. 'Ah, my friends, don't feel happy too soon!' shouted a tall, thin, grey-headed old man who was said to have held a not unimportant position under the Weimar Republic. 'Don't be happy too soon! Wait until the camp gates are torn open, the watch-towers surrounding us pulled down. Even if Hitler is dead, which is by no means sure, a host of kindred spirits still survive—Goering, Himmler, Goebbels and many others—eager to succeed him.'

That night, the news filtered through to us that our great hope had not after all been fulfilled. Our disillusionment and depression were as profound as our hope had been earlier. We no longer held our heads high, as we had done before our hope had been dispelled. Everybody remained silent, for none of us could bring himself to say anything.

The soldiers crept out of their lairs, evil-tempered and vengeful, lashing out at anyone in their path. It was, of course, in order for them to revenge themselves on those who had secretly hoped that the noblest being on earth had been killed.

The Kapos came to themselves and took up the

whips they had earlier laid aside. It was inadvisable to stand too near them, since they, too, were in a vicious mood. They wanted to show their masters that they were loyal servants of the Fuehrer and were prepared, if the occasion called for it, to exact vengeance. In Block 5, the lawyers had nothing to laugh about. They were cruelly beaten up and only a few survived until the next day.

The aged professor in the next room to mine in the hospital barracks was not forgotten either. He had sharply attacked the Fuehrer in his book, so he was dragged from his bunk at midnight and taken away, no one knew where. It was said that only his head was brought back and thrown into the cellars where the corpses lay.

I do not know exactly how many people lost their lives that night as scapegoats for the attempt on Hitler, but they were numerous. Fritz the Kapo disappeared, too, although why he should have done was a mystery. He had always been a faithful servant of Hitler. Was it a mistake perhaps? Nobody will ever know.

The prisoners with a red flash on their prison jackets did not escape unscathed either. Not by any means. The red flash denoted that they had flirted with Marxism at one time or another. They, too, had to pay for the attempt on Hitler's life. The men

176

in the torture cellar were busy, and the lights burned there all night long. It was a veritable night of the long knives, and anyone who descended the cellar steps did not mount them again.

The cobbler Kapo was busy beating up those who had stolen boots and shoes from his store; the clothing storeman punished those who had stolen clothing; the soldier in charge of the kitchen tormented the orderlies who had been so ready to hand out food to the prisoners.

That was what happened on the day that passed into history as the day they tried to kill Hitler—July 20, 1944. Somehow, I lived through that long, terrible twenty-four hours.

TREATMENT

The sick-bay S.S. man disappeared after July 20. The rumour went round that he had become suspect, and some even said that he had been heard to express the hope that the attempt on Hitler's life would succeed. Be that as it may, we never discovered what had happened to him.

The man who replaced him was in the true S.S. tradition. The whip was his method of treatment. Sometimes, exceptionally, someone with lung trouble or heart disease would be admitted to the sick-bay, and the S.S. 'doctor' would give him twenty-five lashes, or more if the fancy took him. When he had finished, he would ask his victim whether he was now cured. Woe betide him if he said no, because the 'doctor' would repeat the 'treatment'. A French doctor among the prisoners dared to voice a mild protest and himself received a flogging. I heard the S.S. man ask him if he had changed his mind about the efficacy of the treatment. The Frenchman agreed that it was an excellent method. If he had not done so, he would have been flogged to death.

Under the new regime, only cases with open

wounds were admitted to the sick-bay. As soon as the wounds had healed the prisoner was sent back to work. One day a prisoner was admitted with a broken arm. How had he broken his arm, the S.S. man wanted to know. The Kapo of Block 8 had done it, the prisoner said. He was ordered to go and get the Kapo.

When the Kapo appeared, the 'doctor' said:

'Why did you break his arm?'

'Because he is lazy.'

'I know that without your telling me. Don't you know a more suitable punishment?'

'There are many, sir. I don't know which one you mean, sir.'

'You don't, eh? Good, I'll show you. Bend over.'

The Kapo was staggered. This was the first time in his career as a Kapo that he had been reprimanded for breaking a prisoner's arm. But even a Kapo had to obey an S.S. officer and he would have to bend over and take a whipping just as a prisoner would have to if the Kapo told him to.

When the S.S. man had given the Kapo twenty-five lashes, he read him a lecture: 'The prisoners are here to work. They must constantly be punished because they are lazy, work-shy parasites, but their punishment must not affect their ability to work. That's what their backsides are for—so that they can be whipped without impairing their ability to work. If, however, you break a prisoner's arm or leg, the Reich has to feed him for a month without getting any work out of him until his arm or leg gets better. That is not in the Reich's interest. Still, if you do happen to break a prisoner's arm or leg, it would be better if you finished him off straight-away. If you had done that, nobody would have found fault with you. Understood?'

'Yes, sir.'

'Dismissed.'

With hanging head, and holding the seat of his trousers, the Kapo slunk out.

Every day at 7.30 in the morning, the S.S. man put on a dazzlingly white coat and began his rounds of the wards. Looking at him, anyone who did not know might well have taken him for an ordinary hospital doctor who would ask each patient how he was progressing, look at a temperature chart here, take a pulse there. But there were no temperature charts and no thermometers in this sick-bay. The sole aim of his daily round was to see which prisoners' wounds had healed over and send them back to work. This 'doctor' did not carry a stetho-scope with him, he carried a whip. Immediately be-hind him came the block clerk with the prisoners' file cards.

Before the S.S. officer entered a ward, prisoners had to take off their bandages and expose their injuries. As he entered the room, the prisoner in charge shouted: 'Attention!' Prisoners had to remain absolutely motionless on their bunks, and nobody was allowed to leave the room, while the 'doctor' strode from bunk to bunk looking at each prisoner's injuries. When he tapped a man with his whip, the clerk took the relevant card out of the pile he carried, and put it to one side. That man would have to be out of the sick-bay by eleven o'clock.

My feet were healed, although I had still not recovered from the effects of lying out in the open in below-freezing temperatures. But none of this was visible, and patients who showed no visible signs of injury were sent back to work. I knew that my only chance of survival lay in remaining in the sick-bay, so I had to find some method of evading the S.S. man's daily inspection.

What I did was to go to the latrine before the round began. The sick-bay had originally been built for the German army, so the latrine was much better than those the working prisoners had to use. Here it was partitioned off into separate compartments with doors that could be bolted. I used to lock myself in one and wait there trembling until the 'doctor's' rounds were over.

Fortunately, the sick-bay routine was not as efficient as it might have been, and prisoners' names or numbers were not called out and checked before the 'doctor' looked at them, so I was able to hide out in the latrine for a considerable time. But then too many other prisoners thought of the same idea, and it became dangerous. On one occasion there were as many as ten of us crammed into a lavatory compartment. If the S.S. man had felt the call of nature, it would have been all up with us. Fortunately, he did not, but the sick-bay Kapo decided that the time had come to take action. Up till then he had turned a blind eye to what we were up to, but now he came and hammered on the door until we opened it and then drove us out of the latrine.

I did not know what to do for the moment, but then I had another idea. Instead of returning to my ward, I went into one the 'doctor' had already visited. I had managed to evade discovery for one more day.

Hiding in the lavatory while the 'doctor' made his rounds was obviously a thing of the past now, but I had no intention of lying on my bunk when the S.S. 'doctor' came round. I had to find some other way of missing him, otherwise I would be sent back to work and that would be the end of me. The ward I was in was the third one he inspected every morning, so, as soon as he had finished in the first one and gone into the second, I used to sneak out of my ward and into the first. There I lay down on a bunk as if I belonged in the ward. I was not always successful, because one prisoner in each ward was responsible for it, and although they were Jews and would not hand me over to the S.S. man, they could not be blamed for not wanting any trouble in their wards and trying to chase me out. But, I had to gain time until the 'doctor' had finished in my ward, so if I was chased out of a strange ward, I always went back, if necessary several times, until the 'doctor' had finished his inspection and I could return to my own ward.

On one occasion, however, my ruse did not work. Nobody would let me stay in another ward, and I became desperate. I dashed along to the 'forbidden room', which was reserved for the S.S. man himself and was usually kept locked. What I was going to do when I got there I did not know, but I had to keep away from my own ward at all costs. God was on my side, however. The key was in the door, and with trembling hands I turned it and went inside. A pistol lay on the table and a large, framed picture of Hitler hung on the wall. By this time I was trembling all over, because the S.S. man would undoubtedly kill me if he found me there. When enough time had passed for him to have finished his inspection in my ward and gone on to the next one, I crept out of the room. To my horror, he was standing in the corridor, but he had his back to me and I was able to slip away unnoticed.

Soon after this an epidemic broke out in the camp. Prisoners began passing blood in their stools, and were reduced to skin and bone within a few days. The camp administration were not particularly bothered until two of the guards also caught the infection. Then they sent for a German army doctor, who recognized the disease straightaway and had the necessary drugs sent to the camp.

The army doctor, a lieutenant, was as good and kind as the S.S. man was vicious and cruel. Although the S.S. 'doctor' was still in charge, the army doctor did all he could to ease our sufferings. Not that he could do very much, because the S.S. were Hitler's own troops and ranked higher than the Wehrmacht, the ordinary army. Consequently, the S.S. man continued to flog those of his 'patients' he felt like flogging. The army doctor toured the camp and sent any prisoner who was seriously ill to the sick-bay. Usually, the S.S. man sent them away again, but sometimes the army doctor managed to prevail on him to let a prisoner stay.

He gave us moral aid, too. He always had a kind
184

word for every prisoner, and it was enough to see his smiling face to feel that perhaps all was not yet lost. He gave us the latest news from the front every day, and our cautious optimism began to grow stronger.

One day a boy was brought into the sick-bay with a bleeding ulcer. His only hope lay in an immediate operation, but this was unthinkable in a concentration camp. No S.S. doctor ever operated unless he wanted to perform an experiment, and in such cases death was the only outcome. But the army doctor said that he was going to operate. The boy was afraid and shouted: 'You want to kill me, you want to kill me!' It took the army doctor a considerable time to convince him that he was really going to save him and not carry out a medical experiment, and the boy only calmed down finally when the doctor promised to look after him personally and see that he was given only light work afterwards. The operation was successful and the boy made a full recovery.

Saturdays were the best days of all in the sickbay. There were no medical rounds then, because the S.S. 'doctor' used to accompany the corpses sent to Mauthausen for burning. The Melk crematorium was still being built, so the corpses had to be sent to Mauthausen. I used to look out of the window every

Saturday morning and watch the S.S. man drive off in the big lorry. One Saturday, however, something went wrong. I had seen the lorry drive off half an hour before and had just settled myself on my bunk, when the S.S. man walked in on his rounds. It was too late to try and leave the room, so I had to lie there and wait for the tap from the whip that meant I would be discharged and sent back to work. Sure enough it came.

By this time, the army doctor no longer came to the sick-bay every day, but only two or three times a week. This time, however, the S.S. man had barely left the ward when the army doctor hurried in to tell him something. I leapt out of my bunk and dashed over to the army doctor.

'Please, doctor, I have heart trouble, but the S.S. man discharged me. Please help me. Please, please help me.' He looked at me pityingly, stroked my shaven head, asked how old I was and put his head to my chest to listen to my heart, which was beating fit to burst. Then he straightened up, made a note of my number and said: 'You will stay here.' As he went out of the room, I wondered whether I would in fact be able to stay. I would have to wait till eleven o'clock to find out, because that was when all discharged prisoners had to leave. Eleven o'clock came and went and I was still there and then the block clerk came in and said: 'Congratulations, lad. You've certainly got plenty of guts. You were lucky this time and it worked, but I wouldn't try it again if I were you, it's too risky. In fact, it's more than your life's worth to resist any decision of the S.S. doctor. Still, as I said, you were lucky, and I heartily congratulate you.'

Everybody admitted to the sick-bay had to give up his clothes and shoes. The shoes were all piled up in the wash-room, to which we had access, and were not returned to their owners when they were discharged. Every so often, the notorious cobbler-Kapo would come and collect the shoes and take them off to his store.

Many prisoners came to the sick-bay every day for minor treatment, and on one occasion I saw a man whose feet were as raw and bleeding as mine had once been. He had some blood-soaked bandages round them, but his attempt to gain admission to the sick-bay was unsuccessful. I went to the wash-room, got a pair of shoes and gave them to him. He was overjoyed and kissed me on the forehead. 'May God repay you for this,' he said. Well, I thought to myself, if it is so easy to do other prisoners a good turn, why shouldn't I hand out shoes to everyone? After all, I knew what it was like to have to go about barefoot.

187

Many of the prisoners reported for treatment in the evenings. They used to stand in a row in the corridor, naked, waiting to be called in one by one. I used to look and see which of them had no shoes and then go and bring some from the wash-room and distribute them. Of course, I had to be careful that nobody else saw me, especially the S.S. 'doctor'. Soon the news was all over the camp—one of the young prisoners in the sick-bay was giving out shoes. The number of prisoners who reported for treatment increased enormously, even if there was nothing wrong with them, just to get shoes. Within a few days there were none left in the wash-room except a few pairs that were totally unwearable.

The cobbler-Kapo was puzzled. He could not understand why there were no good shoes in the wash-room. Unbeknown to me, he decided to lie in wait to see what was happening to the shoes. Inevitably, he caught me in the act of taking a pair one day. 'Aha, now we've caught the shoe thief!' he shouted joyfully, and began hitting me. He banged my head so hard against the wall that my nose started bleeding. The S.S. man was not in the sick-bay at the time, thank God, or that would have been the end of me. The block clerk, hearing the noise, rushed in to see what was happening. 'It is my duty and privilege to punish him, since he committed the crime here in the sick-bay,' he said, dragging me away from the enraged cobbler-Kapo.

'He has got to be finished off!' the Kapo shouted at the clerk.

'Of course he has,' was the reply.

As soon as the cobbler-Kapo had gone, the clerk said: 'You don't deserve my protection after what you've done. I am finally responsible for the shoes and have to answer for anything that goes wrong. I am going to discharge you immediately.' He gave me some clothes and sent me off to Block 7.

Although I knew that I would probably not last long, with my useless hands and feet, I was glad that things had ended the way they had. When I entered the block, I was greeted on all sides by prisoners to whom I had given shoes. Then they saw that I didn't have any myself, but I shrugged off their queries with the remark that: 'All cobblers go bare-foot.'

I was put on the night shift and had to go out to work straightaway. Hopefully, I marched along with the rest, thinking that perhaps we were going to the building site where the superintendent had let me sit in his hut all day. But it was a vain hope. We were taken to a place where we had to move lengths of railway line at the double. My companions estimated that the load per prisoner was

189

about one and a half hundredweight. The Kapo drove us like dogs, lashing about him with his whip and shouting. This went on the whole night.

It was then that I felt for the first time that something was wrong with my lungs. I had difficulty in breathing, and every time I took a breath, there were cracking noises in my chest. My lungs had become infected, although I did not know it at the time.

By 9 o'clock in the morning I was at the end of my tether. My thoughts were full of my schoolfriend, who had had the courage to end it all a week after being sent to this living hell. Then, I had thought his action a sin, but now I envied him for not having to suffer any more as we were all suffering. I decided to follow his example. But what was the best method to use? I had read somewhere that an overdose of sleeping tablets was an easy way to die, but where could one obtain sleeping tablets in a concentration camp?

I rejected the idea of hanging myself. It would mean dying like a criminal and, apart from that, it would be far too painful. I considered and rejected various other possibilities. Slashing the veins in my wrists was not the right method either. Then I thought of an idea. Why not do as my friend had done, and dash myself against the barbed wire? One

190

burst from a watch-tower machine-gun and all my worries would be over. I wriggled backwards off my bunk and reached for my trousers. Then I let go of them. What did I need them for any more? I had just gone out of the hut when a story my grandfather had told me when I was a little child came into my head:

A resourceful young man decided to travel abroad, to a country where diamonds lay in the ground like stones. After all, he thought to himself, if he could come back with only a handful of them, he would be able to live without a care in the whole wide world for very many years. He said good-bye to his young wife, promising to return as soon as he could, unaware, as she also was, that she was pregnant. After a long, dangerous and eventful sea voyage, he landed at his Eldorado. In the meantime his wife bore him a son, but since there was no such thing as a postal service in those days, she had no way of letting him know.

By now he had many more than a handful of diamonds, but he kept deferring his return because the country enchanted him. It became ever more difficult to tear himself away, and as the years passed he thought less and less about returning home. Eighteen years passed and then, one day, he was seized with such home-sickness that he vowed to sail home aboard the next available ship. The feeling of nostalgia soon passed, but he was too religious to break his vow, and took the next ship home.

It was almost midnight when he stood before the door of the house where he had said good-bye to his wife eighteen years before. Standing there, he tried to think how he could enter the house and speak to his wife without frightening her, because she would certainly not recognize him after eighteen years. Suddenly he heard voices inside the house. Carefully, he listened at the door and recognized his wife's voice. She was talking to a man. Raging at her unfaithfulness, he drew his dagger, ready to stab his wife and the man she had betrayed him with. Then he remembered his father's dying words: 'My son, never carry out any drastic decision on the same day as you make it. Sleep on it first.'

He sheathed his dagger, lay on the ground and tried to sleep, but he was too keyed up and tossed and turned all night. In the morning, he heard his wife and the man talking again.

'My dear son,' said his wife, 'you are now eighteen years old and the time has come for you to seek a wife. Your father left me eighteen years ago, not knowing that I was pregnant. Since he has never returned, it is hardly possible that he is still alive. He may even have been drowned on the outward voyage. There is no sense in waiting any longer for him to return.'

'God be praised that he restrained me,' the man exclaimed as he knocked on the door of the house.

I went back into the hut and lay down on my bunk. When the block senior's whistle blew, my resolve was no longer so steadfast. The will to live had triumphed.

I must have been out of my mind, I thought to myself. How could I have entertained so wicked a thought? Had not my teacher told me that I must rejoice in my fate, be it good or bad?

The block senior's rough voice broke into my thoughts. 'Outside!' he shouted. We marched to work at the double, always at the double, in order not to lose a moment of working time. We had to build an aircraft factory to turn out aircraft which would help to make the thousand-year Reich's dream of world domination come true.

This time I had an easy job. Another boy about the same age as myself and I had to dip rusty screws in oil and petrol and clean off all the rust, sitting on the floor in the shed.

The shed was enormous. Several other youngsters had the job of watching to see that none of the prisoners went to sleep on the job. To help them they had long, thin rubber whips. If they found an unfortunate prisoner who had dozed off, they hit him with their whips and drove him over to where a Kapo was waiting to administer the regulation twenty-five lashes with his much thicker whip. He had plenty of work to do, because many prisoners took advantage of the dim light in the shed to lie down and rest for a little while, and most of them fell asleep.

I dozed off more than once, but my work-companion jogged me awake before any of the watchers noticed. Then I dozed off again, and before my fellow screw-cleaner could nudge me, one of the watchers had seen me. 'Get up, get up. Over to the Kapo, come along now!' he shouted, flicking me all the time with his pencil-thin whip. My companion tried to persuade him to let me go this time, but in vain. 'I do my job properly,' he barked. 'I can't make any exceptions.' Of course he did his job properly. He got an extra soup ration for it, and he did not want to jeopardize that for me.

In the end, my companion persuaded him to punish me himself, instead of handing me over to the Kapo. But then another problem presented itself. The Kapo's whip was much thicker than his, so if I ought to receive twenty-five lashes from the Kapo, he himself ought to give me more. After some thought, he decided that fifty lashes with his whip equalled the regulation twenty-five with the Kapo's whip. Even then, he said, I was getting off lightly. The Kapo's whip was four inches in diameter, while his was only the thickness of a man's finger. Furthermore, he said, he could not wield a whip with the force a Kapo would put behind it, and I could not complain if he decided to give me five lashes for every one the Kapo would have given me. However, he would restrict himself to fifty and would allow me to keep my trousers on. He made these concessions, he added, because I seemed to be about the same age as himself and could theoretically have been a school-friend; also, I was not the worst offender.

True, fifty lashes with a thin whip wielded by a boy were probably not as bad as twenty-five delivered by a Kapo, but they were still bad enough. I would be black and blue for a fortnight afterwards and have to lie on my bunk face downwards. Still, it could have been worse.

I was about to stand up and bend over to take my punishment, when a soldier rushed into the shed. It was his job to see that everyone was working, and when he saw the watcher talking to me, he did not know what it was all about. All he could see was that I was not working, and it looked as if the watcher was stopping me from doing so.

Soldiers were not in the habit of asking prisoners many questions, and we were forbidden to speak to them unless they first spoke to us. This one fell upon the unfortunate youngster with the whip, knocked him down and kicked him hard several times. Bloody and groaning, he picked himself up and made himself scarce. We did not see him again until the march back to camp next morning. He would never make another exception for anyone, he swore it. That night's experience had been enough for him, he declared.

Some time after the incident with the soldier, it must have been two o'clock in the morning, I felt an urgent need to go to the latrine. Where we worked, the latrine was primitive in the extreme, just a large deep pit. Many prisoners went there for no other reason than to escape from their back-breaking work for a while. But the guards knew this and kept a strict watch. At first they used to content themselves with flashing torches on the prisoners at the latrine, to make sure that they were really relieving themselves and not malingering. But this was not effective enough. The prisoners had to be so terrified that they would only leave their work when it was impossible for them to delay going to the latrine any longer. There must be no incentive for any prisoner to go there for a rest. So the camp authorities devised a better scheme than making spot checks with torches. Instead, at frequent but irregular intervals, men with whips would appear at the latrine pit and lash out at everybody they found there. This system was almost foolproof. Nobody who did not have to be there was going to go to the latrine and run the risk of a whipping.

I had no alternative, I had to go. I had just crouched down at the edge of the pit, when somebody kicked me hard in the face. I lost my balance and fell headlong into the filth that filled three-quarters of the pit, just managing to get my head above the surface in time. Whoever had kicked me in it—it was too dark to make out whether it was a soldier or a Kapo, but it must have been one or the other—began bombarding me with stones, fortunately without hitting me. Another prisoner who had seen what had happened, gave me his hand and helped me to pull myself out of the stinking, ordure-filled pit. From then on I was fair game for every soldier and Kapo who saw me. Everyone hit me or kicked me, and on the march back to camp the guards continuously hit me with rifle butts.

Back at the camp, my troubles were not yet over.

'Get out of this hut!' the block senior yelled at me. 'You make the whole place stink.' Miserable and desperate as I had been before, my spirits now sank so low that I resolved to commit suicide. This time I meant it with all my heart. Why should I go on living? Rather death than this degradation and foulness and sheer, bowel-twisting misery. Before I threw myself against the electrified barbed wire fence, however, I would say good-bye to my school comrade Levy, in the next hut. Let at least one person from my home village know what happened to me, I thought. When he saw me he just looked. I told him what I intended doing and he made no attempt to dissuade me. I looked at him and saw that he could not last much longer either. He was fourteen years old and looked fifty. All he said was: 'God be with you.'

The fence was about a hundred and thirty yards away. I started running. Ninety yards to go, sixty, thirty. A soldier in one of the watch-towers began training his machine-gun on me. Suddenly, I felt an excruciating pain in the sole of my right foot and sat down abruptly on the ground. A piece of glass had embedded itself in my foot, which was now bleeding profusely. But what did it matter? I would soon bleed much more when the machine-gun bullets from the watch-tower tore into my body.

I struggled to my feet and prepared to run, but something stopped me. Suppose the glass was a sign from heaven? Suppose it had shown me how I could save myself? I picked up the piece of glass, put it in my trousers pocket, and went to the well, where I undressed and washed my clothes and myself. Then I went back into the hut and lay down on my bunk—but not to sleep. I had more important things to do. All night long, I scraped away at my foot with the piece of glass. It was agony, but I had to do it. If I could enlarge the injury enough, I might be able to get back into the sick-bay. After two hours, my foot was bleeding so much that I became frightened. The prisoners always said that mud would stop any bleeding, so I went outside and smeared my foot thickly with mud. The bleeding stopped.

At midday, I dressed and reported to the block doctor. He decided who could report to the sick-bay. After looking at my foot, he told me to report there at six that evening. That meant that I did not have to go out to work. I waited impatiently for six o'clock. Would the S.S. man consider my injury bad enough for him to admit me to the sick-bay? I considered inflicting a wound on my other foot, but gave up the idea. In the final analysis, everything depended on how the S.S. 'doctor' felt. If he did not want to admit me, nothing would make him. If he did, then my right foot was sufficiently badly injured.

At last it was six o'clock. 'Fall in for sick-bay treatment.' About a hundred prisoners queued up outside the sick-bay, all of them naked, as prescribed for sick parade. Inside, five or six doctors were busy bandaging up prisoners who had come for treatment. Eventually it was my turn and I stepped up to the French doctor, a prisoner like me. He would gladly admit any prisoner to the sick-bay, but it did not depend on him. The S.S. doctor had the final say. The Frenchman cleaned up my foot and said: 'All right, you can go.'

I broke out in a cold sweat. 'But, doctor, aren't you going to keep me in?'

'No, I can't,' he replied. 'I have had to turn away far worse cases.'

Unable to help myself, I burst into tears. 'Please, please, doctor, keep me in. I can't stand it out there any more. I am at the end of my tether.'

'I can't, I'm not allowed to, in fact I am under orders here, as you know. The S.S. doctor has the last word. I know him well. He won't admit you with your injury. He refuses to accept people who are far more badly injured.'

I saw that my pleading had been in vain. With a heavy heart I turned to go, but another prisoner, who had observed the whole scene, shouted: 'Kiss his hand, kiss his hand.' I did not understand, but had nothing to lose, so I took the Frenchman's hand and kissed it. He looked at me paternally, stroked my head and considered what to do with me. Finally, he turned to Dr Hirsch and asked, in broken German: 'What diagnosis shall I write down?'

'Injured foot,' said Dr Hirsch.

The Frenchman made a note of my prison number and sent me out into the corridor to await the S.S. 'doctor's' inspection. One of three things could happen. Either I would be admitted, or I would be sent away, or else I would be given twenty-five lashes and then sent away. There were four or five people ahead of me to be whipped, so I had quite a long wait, but finally my turn came.

'What's the matter with you then?' the S.S. doctor yelled at me, sweating like a pig from his exertions. I showed him my foot. 'Well, yes, he can't run.' I had made it! I was a patient again!

The block clerk entered me in his books and I was given a bunk in the same room as I had been in before. The senior patient there, Dr Sebastian, was not too pleased to see me. He was responsible for everything that happened in the room and had every reason for thinking that my continual hiding during medical rounds would eventually result in very unpleasant consequences. He was also very curious as to how I had managed to regain admission to the sick-bay only two days after I had been discharged, since everyone knew how difficult it was to be admitted at all. He asked to see my injuries. 'Don't tell me that such injuries could appear by themselves in two days,' he said, 'I know better than that. Tell that story to the S.S. "doctor". He might believe it, because he knows nothing about medicine.'

The block clerk, too, suspected that my wounds were self-inflicted, but fortunately he kept his suspicions to himself when the S.S. 'doctor' examined me. Afterwards, however, he said to me: 'You're a sly fox.'

'What do you mean by that?' I asked him.

'You know exactly what I mean.'

'I don't understand.'

'Don't tell me that.'

'I really don't know what you mean.'

'I'll tell you then. Those injuries on your foot appeared so suddenly because they were self-inflicted. Not that I'm bothered that you have come back here again. But tell me, how can anyone as religious and God-fearing as you seem to be, practise such deceit?'

'My grandfather often used to visit very old

people, and I went with him on one occasion. It was at the beginning of the war, and my grandfather and the old woman he had come to see—she was over ninety—were discussing the new laws passed against the Jews. Many had lost their livelihood when their businesses had been confiscated, they said. The result was that a big proportion were forced to earn a living by dealing on the black market. The newspapers lost no time in saying that all Jews were black marketeers and never let pass an opportunity of betraying the country. Then my grandfather told the following story:

'There was once a Jewish beggar, who went from village to village, knocking on every door and asking for alms. Once a year, always at the High Holy Days, he went back to his family and gave them all he had collected, for it would have to suffice them for another year, until he came again.

'One day, when he had already started on his way home, he had to pass through a thick forest. Suddenly, he saw a robber with a loaded pistol in his hand, barring his path.

' "Oh please, please, don't shoot," pleaded the beggar. "Have mercy on my small children. After all, you only want my money. Here, take it all, it's yours, I give it to you in all sincerity. Only spare my life, I beg of you."

'The robber was not entirely heartless, so he stole the beggar's money, which had taken him a year to collect, and told him he could go. The beggar thanked him for being merciful, but before he went on his way he said he would like to ask a great favour of the robber.

' "I am sure you would not want me to quarrel with my wife," he told the robber. "However, if I arrive home without a farthing after a year away my wife will give me a terrible scolding. She will never believe that I've been robbed. No, she'll say I've spent the money on drink. You have it in your power to help me."

' "Perhaps you'd like me to give you your money back?" said the robber menacingly.

' "Oh no, such an impertinence would never occur to me. What I had in mind was, if it's no trouble of course, for you perhaps to put a few bullets through my coat if I take it off. When my wife sees that my coat has bullet holes in it, she'll be so pleased I escaped alive she won't worry about the money."

'The robber agreed, so the beggar took off his coat and hung it over the branch of a tree, and the robber shot a few holes in it. "Just a few more, if you don't mind," asked the beggar. The robber obliged. "And some more, please. You see, the more bullet holes there are, the more likely my wife is to believe me." The robber shot so many holes in the coat that when the beggar asked him to fire just a few more shots, "to make it look really convincing", the robber had no ammunition left.

' "Aha, you have no ammunition left, eh?" shouted the beggar. "Give me back my money!"

' "Not for nothing do people say that you Jews are swindlers. Only a Jew could play such a dirty trick!" screamed the robber, enraged.

'The Jew, however, leapt at the robber, gave him a good beating, took back his money and made his escape.'

CONVALESCENCE

Something unusual was afoot. The S.S. 'doctor' began visiting his patients at midday as well as in the mornings at the usual time. What was going on? Before long, we realized that a list was being compiled of all the seriously ill patients. They were to be sent to a convalescent home, rumour said. Then my name was added to the list. I had been in the sick-bay too long.

I nearly went out of my mind with worry. The convalescent home story did not ring true at all. Why should they be making a list of all the very ill prisoners? To send them away, yes, but not, I was sure, to any convalescent home. Later, we learnt that the 'convalescent home' was Auschwitz, one of the most notorious of all the death camps.

What was I to do? This time I could see no way out. The wonder rabbi's prophecy was not going to come true, after all. Then I saw the German army doctor in the corridor. I rushed over to him and told him that I was very worried. 'What about?' he asked.

'The S.S. "doctor" has put me on the list with the seriously ill patients.'

'He's put you on the list? No, it would be a pity to waste such a young life. You must be taken off. What is your number?' He wrote it down and went into the office. I waited in the corridor until he came out. 'You've been taken off the list,' he said.

The next morning, all the seriously ill prisoners were loaded onto army lorries and driven away.

I had escaped almost certain death once more, but only a few days passed before a fresh danger threatened. I had managed to evade the daily medical rounds so far, but then the S.S. 'doctor' went away and the block clerk, who was not an evil man, decided to make the rounds himself. His purpose was quite honourable—he wanted to make room for other prisoners by discharging those whom he judged to be better—but he had no right to do this. He had no medical training and was in no position to tell who was better and who was not. However, he certainly meant well and no blame can be attached to him for his intentions. But I was in danger because he wanted to discharge me. I asked him why, when he knew that it would mean my death. 'You've had a long enough rest here,' was his reply. When I pointed out to him that he had no medical knowledge and could not tell who had recovered and who not, he grew angry and hit me twice on the side of the head. Then he walked away.

207

So I had been vanquished again. I had better be prepared to leave the sick-bay very soon. How ironical that it should not be the cruel and vindictive S.S. 'doctor' who had discharged me, but the block clerk, who was not a cruel man at all. I could see no way of getting round his ruling. But then the clerk had second thoughts. He came into the ward, apologized for hitting me and said: 'What you said was right. I shall ask the army doctor to examine all those I have marked down for discharge, and let him decide.'

When the doctor saw me, he said to the clerk: 'Let the boy stay.'

'If that is your wish, doctor,' replied the clerk and crossed me off the list.

I had been saved yet again.

RETURN TO MAUTHAUSEN

At the end of September, a large number of prisoners were to be transferred to Mauthausen, and I was included among them. Again I sought the army doctor's intercession, but this time he refused to have me crossed off the list. This contingent really was going to the sick quarters at Mauthausen. We were not, as the previous two contingents had been, destined for the gas chambers. When he saw from my face that I did not believe him, he swore that he was telling the truth. Himmler had ordered that there were to be no more contingents of prisoners sent to Auschwitz, he said. Then I was reassured.

The lorries took us off on Jewish New Year's Day. The weather was beautiful and sunny, and helped to raise my spirits. At least we had left Melk behind, I thought. But the sight of Mauthausen soon plunged me back into gloom and misery again.

First we had to have a shower and then we were taken to the sick camp, hardly a hundred yards from the concentration camp proper. Like the concentration camp, the sick quarters were surrounded by an electrified barbed wire fence, and there were the same watch-towers with S.S. men training their machine-guns on us.

The sick camp consisted of eight long wooden huts, with numbers painted on their sides. I was put into Hut 6. We did not have to work, which was a very great advantage, but the rations were extremely skimpy. Still, they were enough to prevent one from dying from starvation.

If things had remained like that, we could have managed to keep our end up, somehow, but they soon changed for the worse. First came the order that we were to be not one prisoner to a bunk but two. Then it was three, then four and then five. Five prisoners to each wooden bunk.

The man next to me in my bunk was a well-known ear, nose and throat specialist from Budapest, Professor Polacsek. He was given special treatment, being allowed to keep his private possessions and receive parcels from Hungary. The professor took very little notice of what was going on around him. For most of the day he sat on the bunk and read a book of psalms, the only book in the camp. Other prisoners said that, before he was forbidden to practise, he used to visit the synagogue before every operation, with the patient's case history under his arm, to pray that the operation would be successful.

Because he was so religious, I could not understand why he was continually saying that he would never survive life in the camp. 'If you believe so strongly in God, why don't you trust in His protection?' I used to ask him. The only answer he ever gave me was to shake his head. When he died, I learnt that he had already been suffering from cancer of the throat when he came to Mauthausen.

In November, a contingent of sick prisoners arrived from Gusen concentration camp, and my friend Zoltan Klein, from Nagykaroly, was among them. He told me that my brother Michael and my cousin Samuel Brach were still alive there. I had a shock when I saw Zoltan, because he had become like a skeleton. He told me how badly the prisoners at Gusen were treated. The concentration camp there was divided into two parts, known as Gusen 1 and Gusen 2. Gusen 1 was no rest home, but what happened at Gusen 2 was so bestial that it beggared the imagination. And this was where my brother and my cousin were.

Zoltan told me that Michael and my cousin were the only two left alive out of the fifty people from my home village who had been sent to Gusen. Even Chief Rabbi Jungreis was dead. My brother and my cousin had a Kapo to thank that they were still alive. Savage and vicious though he was, he had decided to take them under his protection for some reason. But even the healthiest could not last for much more than a month at Gusen. There was no sick-bay there, even as rudimentary a one as at Melk and Auschwitz. Anyone at Gusen who fell ill was locked up in hut 13—and never left it alive. Zoltan told me what happened there. Every night the prisoners, sick men all of them, had to line up and climb onto a chair one by one, while the Kapo, a convicted murderer, stood by and watched. If a man could not get onto the chair at the first attempt, or if his foot so much as twitched when he was on the chair, he was chased into the freezing latrine. There he was forced to lie face downwards on the ice-covered ground while a blanket was thrown over him. Any prisoner who moved his head out from under the blanket had it smashed in with an ice-pick. When the Kapo thought he had enough victims for that night, they were taken one by one and dumped head first into a barrel filled with water.

My friend Zoltan had been lucky enough—if lucky is the word—to be sent to Mauthausen, but he died just the same, of starvation.

TO GUSEN

One day, it must have been about the middle of December, there was a comb-out of prisoners who were fit for work. We all had to report to the camp doctor, Dr Csaplinsky, for him to examine us and decide whether we could be sent out to work or not. My frozen hands looked all right outwardly, and I had no open wounds, so I was declared fit. The very next day I was moved to the concentration camp proper, given a shower and put in a hut. There the block senior told us that we would only be there three days at the most and that we would then be sent to Gusen to the 'mincing machine'. My blood ran cold when I heard the name. Even though my brother and cousin were there, I had no wish to join them. But I had no alternative.

On the morning of the fourth day, we heard the block senior shout: 'Gusen contingent fall in at once.' I started trembling all over and my heart pounded in my chest. I felt as if I could not breathe, came over faint and crumpled to the ground. The block senior dashed over in a fury and started kicking me, yelling at me to get up. The block clerk came over to help and began belabouring me with what felt like a wooden truncheon.

According to their lights, I suppose they had reason to be angry. 499 prisoners out of a contingent of 500 were ready to march off, while the five-hundredth was holding up the proceedings by feeling faint and falling to the ground. The S.S. men were waiting with their machine-guns to escort us to our destination, and the S.S. were notoriously impatient at being kept waiting.

Eventually, the block clerk realized that I could not get up, however hard he hit me. The other prisoners would have to move off without me. But this would entail a lot of work. The camp books would have to be corrected, since they said that 500 prisoners had been sent to Gusen and, in fact, only 499 had been sent. The soldiers at the gate would have to be told, too, and the commandant at Gusen would have to be telephoned and informed that he would be taking delivery of 499 prisoners not 500.

I was left lying on the floor in the hut for well over an hour. Then a doctor appeared, took one look at me and said: 'Heart palpitations.' But I felt better after a while and my heart-beats returned to normal. When the block senior came back he said: 'You bloody swine! You caused a right mess, you did!' Then he added: 'You didn't miss anything by not going to Gusen.' As if I did not know that!

It was decided to send me back to the sick camp,

and in the early afternoon a prisoner appeared with a handcart normally used for transporting corpses, dumped me on it and took me back to the sick camp. Zoltan was overjoyed to see me and learn how I had missed being sent to Gusen. 'You have escaped certain death, and I congratulate you,' he said.

THREE WEEKS OF
STARVATION

The Allied armies were advancing rapidly, so more and more of the concentration camps with which the now shaky thousand-year Reich was so richly endowed, had to be evacuated. Since all available means of transport were reserved for the troops, prisoners from evacuated concentration camps had to proceed on foot in the bitter winter cold. Most of the poorly clad prisoners succumbed on the march, but even those who reached their destinations alive were unable to work, because their limbs were frozen.

As the number of evacuated camps grew so, naturally, the number of other camps the prisoners could be sent to declined, and they became even more crowded than before. Once more the order was given: Five prisoners to a bunk. Each bunk was only two feet wide, so it was inevitable that prisoners should have to lie partly on each other, and the hut resounded with the cries and shrieks of sick men in pain who could not even lie down properly.

The camp authorities decided that they would have to put an end to this unbearable situation. A commission of high-ranking S.S. officers appeared in the camp in order to consider possible solutions, and they decided on special measures to ease the shortage of accommodation. What had been the practice at an earlier time, namely machine-gunning prisoners, was out of the question now because every belt of ammunition was needed at the front. Instead it was decreed that not a single ounce of bread would be distributed to any of the sick prisoners for three weeks and the ration of watery soup would be cut from one and a half pints to half a pint. To hasten things along, salt would not be added to the soup.

Results were not slow in showing themselves. In one hut alone, prisoners began dying at the rate of sixty a day. This meant that, in the eight huts making up the sick camp, nearly five hundred prisoners were dying every day, apart from those who died in the actual concentration camp itself.

There are no words in any language to describe the sufferings of the starving prisoners, but at least there was one small consolation, if it can be so described—dying was easy. One would be talking to a fellow prisoner when, suddenly, his eyes would turn up and he would fall to the ground. It had happened, he was dead. We all felt as if we were already in the ante-chamber of heaven. When any of us took leave of a friend, or even an acquaintance, we always said: 'See you in heaven,' or, 'Have a good journey to heaven.'

Yet, remarkably, our spirits were not as oppressed and desolate as might have been expected. There were plenty of artists, singers, writers and other creative people among us and they knew well how to lighten the atmosphere and ease the way for those who awaited the imminent coming of the angel of death and his myrmidons. We even joked about our desperate situation. Nobody was dying anywhere else in the world, we said, because the angel of death was so busy at Mauthausen that he had no time to attend to anybody else. We even made up a song about it.

I had grown as thin as a skeleton and expected the angel of death to come for me at any time. One by one, my friends and acquaintances had died, and now I was alone among hundreds of starving, dying strangers.

It must have been our fifteenth or sixteenth day without bread that the miracle happened. I was lying on my bunk, absorbed in my thoughts, when I heard someone calling my name. I could not understand it, because prisoners were always referred to by their numbers, not their names. I stood up with the greatest difficulty and reported to the Kapo who was looking for me. He took me to the block senior's room, where an S.S. man was waiting. I was so bemused that I forgot to click my heels, but quickly pulled myself together and remedied the omission. The S.S. man looked me searchingly up and down and then asked me, in Hungarian, where I came from, who my father was, and so on. Finally, he told me that he came from a neighbouring village, knew my father and had been friendly with my uncle. He was of German origin and had joined the S.S. Now, he told me, he wanted to help me.

There was no need to tell him what help I needed most. He had only to look at my naked body to see. In the sick camp all prisoners were naked. We were not even given a shirt. He gave me a whole loaf of bread and promised to help me further.

After that he came every two or three days, but only for three weeks. At the end of that time he was sent to the front, and that was the end of his help. Veteran prisoners who knew him well were amazed at what he had done for me, because he was known for being anything but kind. Indeed, he was said to have been personally responsible for killing hundreds of prisoners. Be that as it may, the bread he had given me every two or three days for three weeks had helped me to regain a little strength, and now I was less likely to starve to death.

MIDNIGHT PARTY

One night towards midnight, we were all dragged out of our bunks by a group of a dozen or so drunken S.S. men. They seized hold of us, passed us on from one to the other and threw us out of the hut into the snow-covered camp compound. Then I felt myself being picked up off the ground and hurled onto a waiting lorry, standing there with its engine running. As soon as there were thirty or forty prisoners packed into it, it moved off in the darkness. A few minutes later it stopped in front of a house, and we were all pushed off the lorry and forced inside.

We found ourselves in a big, beautifully decorated room filled with shouting S.S. men and their scantily clad girl friends. Some of them wore masks and others were so thickly larded with make-up as to make their faces unrecognizable.

One of the S.S. men jumped up onto the table and shouted: 'There, look at this naked rabble. They made it their business to dishonour German girls.'

Another S.S. man leapt up and bawled at a prisoner: 'How many German girls have you raped?'

'None. I have never been to Germany,' was the

reply. The S.S. man started hitting the prisoner round the head and shouting at him.

'You damn liar!' he yelled, raining blows on the defenceless man in front of him. Then he asked again: 'How many German girls have you raped?' This time the prisoner said, 'Two,' but this still did not satisfy the S.S. man, who went on hitting him until he agreed that he had raped ten German girls.

The next prisoner thought to escape a beating, so when he was asked the same question he said, 'Twenty.' But the S.S. men were out for blood and a crowd of them jumped on him, threw him to the floor and simply kicked him to death.

Some of the girls gleefully joined in the mêlée. Then, suddenly the light went out. Bottles, glasses, plates, ashtrays hurtled through the air, and the drunken shouting of the S.S. men mingled with the screams of the prisoners. The table was overturned and I was knocked flying. As I hit the floor, I felt a broken glass crunch into my thigh.

Round me on the floor prisoners lay dead and injured, and then I saw an S.S. man preparing to jump on me. But one of the girls barred his way and said: 'Oh leave the boy alone.'

By the time it was all over, only ten or twelve of us were able to make our way back to the camp.

TEMPTATION

By the middle of February, starvation was again staring me in the face. In the bunk above me was an old man, an exceptionally lucky fellow with no fewer than twenty-three gold teeth. Never in his wildest dreams, I am sure, had he imagined that these twenty-three gleaming false teeth would save his life.

The block senior, a German political prisoner, was not short of bread and other food, since he had various means of acquiring whatever he fancied. As the old man with the gold teeth felt himself growing weaker and weaker with hunger, he had an idea. He had his gold teeth knocked out of his mouth one by one and bartered them for bread with the block senior. Every day, he handed over a tooth and received a loaf of bread in exchange.

The five of us who shared a bunk had so arranged matters that four of us sat on the floor for several hours at a time while the fifth got a chance to stretch out on the bunk in comparative comfort. One day, when it was my turn to lie down, I noticed that a loose board in the bunk above me had shifted to one side and half a loaf was sticking out through the hole. It belonged to the lucky possessor of the gold teeth, and he had obviously hidden it under his straw palliasse. As soon as I saw the bread, I wanted it with a fierce and burning longing. I had already stretched out my hand to take it and my mind was already busy with the thought of how it would taste. I was rejoicing at having at last found something with which to stave off the pains of hunger, when my conscience came to life. 'No, no,' I said to myself. ' "Thou shalt not steal!" God ordained in the Ten Commandments.'

But it was not so easy. My mind became a welter of confused thoughts and contradictory arguments. On the one hand, my hunger drove me to want to seize the bread quickly and swallow it down while I had the chance. On the other hand, my conscience forbade me to do such a thing. Back and forth swayed my mental tug-of-war, with the advantage now to one side, now to the other. Finally, I could stand it no more. I seized the bread, got out of the bunk, climbed onto the one above and held the half-loaf out to the old man: 'Here, take it, it's yours,' I said. He quickly took the bread from me and looked at me in amazement. After all, he knew that we were all on the brink of starvation, he said, but he would never have believed it possible that anyone in such dire straits would behave in so direct and honest a manner. He broke off half the bread and gave it to me as a reward. I had never before accepted any kind of reward for something I had done for somebody else, but in the circumstances I could not refuse. It is no exaggeration to say that in my whole life I have never been faced with so great a temptation as there in Mauthausen, when all I had to do to get some bread to assuage my raging hunger was to stretch out my hand and take it. Not for nothing do we pray every day: 'God, please shield me from temptation.'

THE RUSSIAN SERGEANT

At the end of February another transport of sick people arrived from Gusen concentration camp. I was overjoyed to see my cousin Sami Brach among the arrivals and learn from him that my brother was alive in Gusen. Sami was put in the same hut as myself, but we had to part after a few days. I had contracted some sort of skin disease and the block doctor pronounced it infectious. Block 8 was reserved for those with infectious diseases, so I was transferred there.

Some very remarkable things were going on in Block 8. Eighteen healthy young people enjoyed extraordinarily good conditions there, while the rest of the inmates were crowded together, four to each narrow bunk. The youngsters had a bunk each, and I frankly admit that I envied them fiercely. While many prisoners starved to death every day, the privileged ones had as much milk and food as they wanted. From the very first day it was a puzzle to me why this group was called the 'Punishment Company', and it was my dearest wish to become a member of it.

Great was my joy when, one day, my three

bunk-companions were moved away and I had the whole two-foot width of the bunk to myself. I felt like a king. I could stretch my limbs now, like a cat when it wakes up after a nap. I pondered deeply over the reason for my sudden, joyous preferment, but could find no explanation.

Early in the afternoon the brother of the block senior, Hans the Kapo, appeared and sat down on the edge of my bunk. Before he said anything he put a large helping of bread in front of me. As can be imagined, my heart thumped with joy at this unexpected gift. I looked at my 'host', who was smiling a tight, secretive smile. His yellowish, almost grimacing face looked back at me frighteningly. He stared at me for some time with his little cat's eyes and then said: 'Ah, what a pity it would be for a nice boy like you to starve to death in misery! I have decided to look after you as if you were my own child. After all, I am a Kapo and the block senior's brother, and I have opportunities for keeping you supplied with enough food.'

Even though I knew only too well the significance of the green flash on his jacket—that he was being held in the camp for murder—he soon gained my confidence and I felt too happy to grasp the horrible significance of his promises. He sat there and talked for hours, mostly about his experiences during the

226

seven years he had spent in prison. One of his stories was so interesting that I have decided to retell it here:

'A Russian sergeant, a prisoner-of-war, was obsessed by thoughts of escape, and night after night he pondered on how he could get hold of a weapon. One day, his chance came. He was working outside the concentration camp on a small building site guarded by S.S. men. A German civilian engineer was in charge of the work.

'With his sharp eyes the sergeant soon saw that the engineer was carrying a pistol in the breast pocket of his jacket. The Russian waited for the engineer to take off his jacket and put it down somewhere. For many months the sergeant waited until, one burning hot August day, he saw that the engineer was walking about without his jacket. Evidently the heat had been too much for him. The Russian began looking for the jacket. He could not see it anywhere, and decided that it must be in the workshop. He peeped through the small window and, sure enough, there it was. The workshop was empty and, after he had made sure that nobody was watching, he took the pistol, some ammunition and 400 marks out of the jacket pocket.

'The sergeant had not yet worked out a detailed escape plan, so the first thing to do was to hide the pistol as quickly as possible. With his fingers he dug a hole in the soft soil, put in the pistol and money and covered them over. He had hardly done so, when the enginner noticed that his pistol was missing and began running backwards and forwards, looking for it. All the prisoners were lined up and thoroughly searched. No reason was given and the sergeant was the only prisoner who knew the secret.

'During the next few days there were quite a number of searches, and the Russian realized that he would have to wait until the incident had been completely forgotten before he could retrieve his booty.

'One day, when the theft had long gone out of everybody's mind, the Russian sergeant retrieved the pistol. He had worked out his escape plan down to the tiniest detail, and his first objective was the S.S. guard whose sentry post was out of sight of the rest of his comrades. Pistol in hand, the sergeant advanced on the Nazi and ordered him to hand over his machine-gun. Had the man refused, the sergeant would have had to shoot him, and that would have been the end of his escape, because the sound of a shot would have brought the other guards running. Fortunately, however, the S.S. man was scared to death and handed over his machine-gun. In a flash, the Russian had removed the magazine from the gun and grabbed the rest of the ammunition. Then he returned the now useless weapon to the S.S. man.

'He could have walked quietly away, but if he had done so, the S.S. man would have alerted his comrades. Apart from that, the sergeant could hardly walk about in broad daylight dressed in his striped prison garb. He would have been stopped at the next corner.

'What he did was to order the S.S. man to accompany him, pointing the machine-gun at him as if he were under escort.

'The timing of the escape attempt had also been extremely carefully worked out. The guards relieved each other every four hours, and the Russian had put his plan into operation immediately after the guard had been changed. This meant that four hours would elapse before it was discovered that the S.S. man was missing.

'The Russian and his "escort" walked on, through woods, across fields, until darkness fell. The time had finally come to get rid of the S.S. man. But how? The sergeant did not want to shoot him, not out of pity, but because to do so would almost certainly mean a death sentence if he were recaptured. On the other hand, he could not just let him go, because he would give the alarm at the nearest police station.

229

In the end, he took the S.S. man into a thick forest and tied him to a tree. Then he ran off.

'He ran all night, stopping only twice. The first time he assuaged his hunger with apples and pears from an orchard, and the second time he broke into a house to steal some clothes.

'As the morning star rose in the sky he came to a lonely hut on a hill. The hut was two-thirds full of hay, so he lay down on it and made himself comfortable. It was a Sunday morning, and the escaped prisoner counted on the farmer staying at home for his Sabbath rest. As he stretched himself out in the hay, he felt something hard underneath him, pulled it out and saw that it was a big sack, filled with smoked meat. He attacked it ravenously and ate until he could eat no more. Then he lay down to rest, his loaded pistol ready beside him.

'He was not left in peace for long. Soon, somebody pulled the door open noisily. The Russian was frightened and reached for his gun. As he did so he saw a grey-haired old farmer standing in the doorway, even more frightened than he was himself.

' "Now I am really in trouble; now they have fixed me," moaned the farmer. "Please, please don't hand me over to the hangman. Three of my sons have died a hero's death and the fourth is fighting at

230

the front. A jealous neighbour has betrayed me. I have a good idea who it was, the old witch. Yes, my wife always warned me to be careful. 'When you kill a pig,' she said, 'be careful his damned mate doesn't get wind of it.' ''

'The Russian had grasped the situation in a moment. He spoke excellent German, so he said to the farmer: "Look, I'm as fed up with this rotten war as you are. Let me lie low here till the end of the war, and you will have nothing to fear." "Gladly, gladly," replied the peasant. "I hope you mean what you are saying and will not set another trap for me and afterwards report me for what I have said."

' "I swear that I am in earnest," the Russian said. "All right then, come with me. There are plenty of places on my farm where you can hide in peace until the war is over. You don't have to worry about food either. As you can see, there is plenty of that here too."

'The sergeant was "adopted" by the family and lived with them for months, undiscovered by anyone outside the household. But for an unlucky chance, he could have stayed there until the end of the war.

'One day the electricity supply in the house failed, and since the family usually tried to avoid calling strangers to the house, the sergeant decided to try

231

and repair the fault himself, climbing onto a ladder near the door to get a closer look at the wiring.

'Now, it so happened that a soldier from the neighbouring village, who was serving in the same unit as the farmer's son, had come home on leave, and he chose this particular moment to come over to the farm to bring greetings from the farmer's son.

'He walked through the doorway just as the Russian had started fumbling with the wires, and when the Russian caught sight of his uniform, he thought the soldier was looking for him, drew his pistol and made to fire. But the German was too quick for him. He did not have time to draw his own weapon, so he kicked the ladder over. As the sergeant fell, his pistol went off, but without hitting anybody. Then the soldier started kicking him. At that moment the startled farmer appeared. He realized at once what had happened and set about calming the two men. But it was too late. The neighbours had heard the shot and sent for the police. That was the end of the sergeant.'

Hans the Kapo took his leave, saying: 'I'll come and see you again tonight.'

The young members of the Punishment Company began dishing out supper and I asked one of them what was so special about them. 'Oh, nothing much. We are the block seniors' boy friends.' So that was it! I began trembling in all my limbs and did not know what to do.

As soon as darkness fell, the Kapo appeared again. I jumped backwards off my bunk and dashed into the compound. The snow came above my knees and I soon collapsed exhausted. For a short time I even dozed off, but the cold was too intense for me to fall into a deep sleep. Apart from that, I was afraid I would freeze to death, because I was stark naked, so I had no alternative but to go back to the hut. When I went inside I saw Hans crouching by the small coal stove. His yellowish face with its forced smile looked positively ghoulish in the meagre light thrown by the oil lamp. I hurried past him and lay down on my bunk. I could not sleep a wink all night for fear that the sinister Kapo would come back. But he never did.

Every day at noon, the kitchen sent in a big cauldron of thick barley soup, and Hans the Kapo shared it out. I decided to stand in the queue and chance my luck. When I came level with him, he looked at me thoughtfully, apparently deciding whether or not to give me any. Finally, he filled his ladle and poured the soup into my bowl. For the whole of the fortnight I was in that hut, the daily performance with the soup was repeated, and I began to gain strength. But then the doctor declared me fit and I had to

233

leave the hut and return to Block 6 and a daily ration of one and three-quarter ounces of mouldy bread and a bowl of 'soup' that was mainly water. I slowly began to lose strength again.

Every day and all day the Allied aircraft circled overhead, and every day the danger of death by starvation increased. Then: 'All those who consider themselves fit to work fall in in the compound.' The shouted order echoed round the camp. I thought it was better to try and work than just stay where I was and die of hunger. After all, I thought to myself, prisoners who work probably get better food.

An S.S. man was seated at a table in the compound, and all the work candidates had to file past him. He took one look at me, standing there all skin and bone, and almost collapsed with laughter. 'Oh yes. You are fit to work, all right! You could become a champion heavyweight boxer! Are you fit?'

'Yes, fit as a fiddle.'

'All right, if you think so. Accepted!'

REUNITED WITH MY BROTHER

When my cousin Samuel discovered that I had reported that I was fit enough to be discharged, he also said that he was fit for work, in order not to be separated from me. I told him that only the future would decide whether or not I had taken the right decision in getting myself discharged from the sick camp, and that the chances of survival there might be better than in the camp proper. But he insisted on remaining with me, whatever happened. 'I am convinced that you will survive,' he added. 'So many miracles have happened to you, that I am certain Providence will not desert you now. In view of this, I feel it right to remain at your side.'

The original concentration camp was full, so we were transferred to a tented camp the Nazis had put up close by. There were no bunks in the huge tents, and we had to lie on the bare ground. But I had been right in my supposition about the rations. Although still very meagre indeed—three and a half ounces of bread a day—they were still double what we had been getting in the sick camp. On the other hand, we were in danger of freezing to death, although it was already the middle of April, since we had neither bunks nor blankets. But Providence was on my side.

Members of the Jewish labour corps conscripted by the Hungarian army and taken over by the Germans began streaming into our tented camp, and they were allowed to keep the things they had brought with them. Among them I discovered a distant relative of mine, a certain Mr Berkovits, who had an enormous quilted bed coverlet. Every night he allowed my cousin Sami and myself to crawl under it with him and keep warm that way. Not only this, but on the march to the camp he had picked all sorts of greenstuff and stowed it away in his rucksack, and now he shared it with Sami and me, giving us both a ration to chew every day.

On our fourth day under canvas, our tent was hit by a bomb, which killed four prisoners and injured very many more. Luckily, Mr Berkovits, Sami and I escaped unhurt.

On our eighth day the notorious death camp at Gusen was evacuated and its few living inmates sent to our tented camp. Among them, to my indescribable joy, was my brother Michael. He looked quite well and was in better physical shape than Sami and me. Having seen the condition I had been in in Auschwitz, he was amazed to find me still alive.

We did not have to work, because there were no longer any working parties, and we just sat about all day exchanging experiences. Everyone was deeply perturbed when all the non-Jewish prisoners were removed. All sorts of rumours swiftly went the rounds, such as that we were all going to be shot or that the camp was going to be set on fire with us inside it. When a lorry loaded with cans of petrol arrived, we were panic-stricken. The guards drove everyone inside the tents and warned us that anyone attempting to go outside would be shot. We were certain now that the camp was to be set on fire. Many prisoners recited the prescribed prayer for when death is near, and composed themselves to die.

But that same day, the cans of petrol were loaded onto the lorry again and taken away and we breathed a little more easily. We were allowed to go outside the tents again and discovered how close we had been to a ghastly death. A passing S.S. man shouted to us: 'You're lucky. Everything was ready to send you all up in smoke, but the order was countermanded at the last moment.'

DEATH MARCH

One day towards the end of April, we heard the shouted announcement: 'The camp is being evacuated. All sick prisoners and those too weak to march report to tent Number 1. The rest muster at the camp entrance.' Uniformed S.S. men with rifles and machine-guns at the ready were already waiting there.

My brother, my cousin and I sat down on the ground in the camp compound and discussed whether to march with the rest or report to tent Number 1. They both asked my opinion, since I was the oldest, so I said: 'It is well-known that sick prisoners who stay behind when a camp is evacuated are often killed. We also know that those who can't keep up with the main body when the march has begun are shot. Nevertheless, I suggest that we go, not stay.' The other two agreed.

I was the weakest of the three. I had been reduced to a walking skeleton, and my shins were no thicker than a man's thumb. My skin was transparent, and all my bones showed through, but still I had decided to march out with the rest, because I was sure that those who stayed behind would be killed.

We got up and went towards the camp entrance, where thousands of prisoners were already drawn up in fives. Every few minutes, a group of a hundred prisoners marched out of the camp and our turn came eventually. It was a beautiful spring day.

As we trudged along, we saw dozens of corpses hanging from telegraph poles. They were German soldiers who had deserted or broken under fire. Each dangling corpse had a notice pinned to it: 'I was a coward', or 'I deserted my unit', or 'I was a traitor'.

Allied aircraft circled overhead, and it seemed as if they knew who we were, because they did not attack us. The roadside was lined with the bodies of prisoners who had been unable to keep up the pace of the march and been shot in the back of the neck.

My feet felt as heavy as lead, and I could barely lift them off the ground, but my brother and my cousin supported me, forcing me to keep marching. I besought them to leave me in peace. I had had enough of life and wanted to die. 'You must keep going,' my brother shouted at me. 'The war is almost over. It would be shameful to die now.'

At sunset, the column halted and we were told that we could lie down to rest. As I collapsed on the ground, I sank into thick mud, but I did not care. At least it was soft. It was over a year since I had slept in a warm bed and was no longer so demanding as to expect one.

All during the night shots rang out and prisoners died, but when morning came, my brother, my cousin and I were still alive. I would have stayed there in the mud, but my brother pulled me to my feet, shouting that I must continue the march. If I had had the strength, I would have pushed him away, but I was as weak as a kitten, so I allowed myself to be dragged off between them, my head sunk on my chest and my feet dragging along the road.

I cannot remember what the scenery was like. I cannot even recall whether the landscape was flat or mountainous, or what kind of trees grew there—indeed, whether there were any trees at all. One thing I do remember, though. As we marched on towards our destination, wherever it might be, a grey-haired, toothless, hunch-backed, old peasant woman came running out of a low, yellow-washed farmhouse and held out a cup of milk to me. I tilted my head back and poured it gratefully down my throat. As I gave her back the empty cup, I heard one of our S.S. escorts shout at her angrily: 'That was a damned liberty! Poor Aryan children can't get enough to eat or drink, yet you come running out and give some milk to a filthy, stinking Jew!'

240

The effect of the milk was astounding. My heart began to beat more strongly, my feet felt lighter, and I was able to move forward unaided. My grandfather's prediction that I would live through the war was coming true, my brother declared. 'Pull yourself together, you will survive,' he said.

My cousin Sami was full of thoughts of escape. 'I've got the feeling that they are going to take us somewhere and then kill us. I suggest we run away.' I could see that my brother also wanted to run away, but I was too weak to do so and he did not want to desert me. 'If you want to try and escape, don't hold back because of me,' I told him.

'No, I won't leave you,' he replied. Then he told Sami: 'But if you have a chance of escaping, take it. Nobody knows where it is safest, but I'm staying with my brother.'

'All right, I'm going to have a try,' said Sami. He took the metal band with his prison number on it off his arm and gave it to my brother. 'If something happens to me and you come through all right, give this to my father as a keepsake, if he's still alive.' My brother put it in his trousers pocket. Sami kissed us both in farewell. He was not going to run away until an opportunity presented itself, but when it did, there would be no time for farewells.

His father and older brother had been in Budapest when the deportations started and had not been
taken, so there was a chance that they were still
alive. However, Sami knew that his mother and
two small sisters were dead, because he had seen
them at Auschwitz when they were sent to join the
queue of those to be gassed because they were unfit
for work.

My brother owed his life to Sami. They had been
at Gusen together and had both worked in the
kitchen there. One day, my brother was peeling
turnips, when he was caught red-handed putting a
piece of turnip in his mouth. Everyone knew that
stealing even the smallest scrap from the kitchen
meant death. The Kapo who had caught him took
him to the wash-room to carry out the sentence.
Sami, who even in his schooldays had had a reputation for dare-devil courage, lost no time. He
picked up a short iron bar lying about the kitchen,
hid it under his shirt and dashed off to the wash-
room. He was none too soon. My brother was
already lying on the floor and the Kapo was just
raising his boot to kick him in the throat. Sami
leapt at the Kapo and hit him hard on the back of
the neck. As the Kapo fell to the ground unconscious, Sami hit him again, several times. When my
brother came to, Sami and he went back to the

kitchen and carried on with their work. The Kapo was dead, much to the delight of the prisoners, who had hated and feared him because of his merciless cruelty, but the S.S. men at the camp made no attempt to find out who had killed him. As far as they were concerned, he was just another dead prisoner. The other Kapos paid him the honour of themselves throwing his corpse into the cellars.

My brother said that it had also been rumoured that they put his whip in his hand and that his body had gone to the crematorium with it still clutched in his dead fingers. He had apparently told his colleagues on one occasion that, if he should be killed, they should murder twelve prisoners in front of his corpse, for revenge. But his successor did not fulfil this wish. He could already see that the war was not going so well for the Germans and considered discretion to be wiser than over-diligence.

We spent the night on a wooded hill-top. But the ground was rock-hard and I could not sleep a wink. The mud of the night before had been a thousand times better. I was glad when dawn came and it was time to move off.

My brother had grown much weaker. He had eaten nothing for two days, and when he got to his feet, he reeled like a drunken man. I decided that I could no longer let him help me along. He was too weak and it would be endangering his life. He argued with me, but gave in when I swore that I would not move from the spot unless he agreed that we should part company. Seeing that I meant what I said, he went on his way.

That day, conditions were a little easier, in that any prisoner who lagged behind the marching group he was in was allowed to join the following group, instead of being shot, as during the first two days of the march. There was a distance of a hundred yards or so between the groups, so that prisoners who dropped behind and found themselves in the open space between the two groups were not under the eyes of the guards at all. But at the rear of the last group there was an S.S. man, and he shot anybody who dropped out of it.

At the start of the day's march I was near the front of the second group. I could not keep up the pace, however, and soon dropped back to the third group and then the fourth. As I was passing from one group to the next, we came to a part of the road bordered by a thick forest. It was an ideal opportunity to make a break for freedom, since none of the guards could see me, but I did not have the strength. Then I saw my cousin Sami. He looked to the rear and to the front, saw he was unobserved, embraced and kissed me and then disappeared into the forest. He was soon lost to sight, but then I heard him shout: 'God keep you.'

'And you,' I shouted back.

THE EXECUTIONER AND
THE WONDER RABBI

In the afternoon it started to rain and a fierce wind came up. My steps grew more and more laggard, and soon I found myself in the last group. I would have to keep up now, for fifty yards behind me was the blond S.S. man who shot any stragglers he saw. I could already see the first houses of Wels, which was only a couple of miles from the camp which was our final destination. If I could last out those two miles, I might still have a chance of saving my life. But I had grown so weak now that the odds against my being able to carry on seemed over-whelming.

As we marched over the bridge across the Danube in Wels, I had to fall out. My heart was beating like a trip-hammer, I felt as if I was choking and my feet refused any longer to obey me. I looked behind me and saw the S.S. man about forty yards away. He was just about to shoot a straggler in the back of the neck. Even as I looked, a shot rang out. Another life ended, I thought. Soon it would be my turn. There were only five or six prisoners behind me, and then . . . I leant against the side of the bridge and said 'Vidu', the prayer before death. Another shot assailed my ears. In my mind's eye I saw my grandfather's face. 'You will survive,' he was saying, 'You will survive.' He was a good man and had never spoken an untruth in his life. God would surely make his prediction come true. Whatever else had been taken from me, I had never lost my trust in God.

Standing there on the bridge, leaning exhaustedly against the balustrade, I must have fallen asleep on my feet momentarily, for I saw the wonder rabbi standing there. He shook me by the shoulder and said: 'This is no time for sleeping. You must act.' 'What can I do?' I asked him. 'My legs refuse to carry me.' 'Climb onto the lorry,' he replied.

I was about to ask him what he meant, when there was a tremendous bang immediately behind me. I opened my eyes and saw an army lorry moving at speed onto the bridge. One of its tyres had burst and it skidded to a halt so close to me that its side brushed my trousers. Was this the lorry the rabbi had meant? I heard another shot and went round to the back of the lorry. Three soldiers were sitting there with a dog. It hardly seemed possible that they would let me get in, but what did I have to lose? 'Please, please,' I begged, 'take me with you.

If you don't, that man there,' I pointed to the S.S. man, 'will shoot me.'

The soldier with the dog gave me a long hard look and then said: 'Jump in.' I tried to climb up, but was too weak. He seized me by my clothes and pulled me into the lorry just as the blond S.S. man came up and yelled at me. 'Come on, Jew, get out of there!' I looked imploringly at the soldiers, and one of them said: 'The lieutenant said he could stay.' The S.S. man must have held a lower rank than the non-existent lieutenant and 'orders is orders'. He turned away and busied himself with some other unfortunates. I heard his pistol crack out again and again.

The lorry's burst tyre was changed and we drove off. Nobody said anything to me, but each of the soldiers gave me something—the first a tin of meat, the next a piece of black bread and the third a small jar of jam.

The lorry stopped at the edge of a thick forest, and one of the soldiers jumped quickly out. Lifting me down, he pointed to the forest, meaning: 'There is the camp.' Then he jumped back into the lorry, which drove off at speed.

About half a mile away, I could see the little village of Gunskirchen, but there was no sign of any camp. The sky was leaden, and it was pouring with rain. I stood and licked at the jam the soldier had given me. Gradually, my heart beats returned to normal and I tried to make my way into the forest. It was a laborious task and I made slow progress. Lifting each foot out of the mud taxed my remaining strength to the full, and I soon lost my heavy wooden clogs.

After an hour or more of this snail's progress, I came upon a group of shouting, cursing, fighting S.S. men. Nobody noticed me in the mêlée. They were arguing whether, now that the war was in its last hours, so to speak, it was wise to kill so many prisoners. 'The Fuehrer's orders must be obeyed at all times!' some of the Nazis were shouting.

I slipped away unobserved, and found myself at the edge of a long, deep mass grave. I stared in horror and my blood ran cold. Had the grave been filled with thousands of corpses, my horror would not have been so great, because I had grown accustomed to such sights. But here, the bodies still moved, still breathed. I wanted to shout aloud so that the whole world would hear me: 'Send the politicians here. Let them negotiate and take their decisions at the edge of this grave. Their conclusions would be quite different from those they reach in gilded conference halls, surrounded by deferential servants!'

But I remained silent, and sat down wearily on one of the logs which lay about the clearing in profusion. All round me prisoners, supervised by S.S. men, were busy pouring lime on the bodies in the grave. One day, a marble tombstone would be erected here, saying: 'Here rest the bodies of more than 10,000 martyrs.'

Suddenly, a powerful S.S. man caught sight of me. 'Hey, you there, skeleton, you belong in that grave!' he shouted, picked me up as if I were a doll, and hurled me towards the grave, where the lime was bubbling and seething. But he misjudged his throw, and I landed on the far side. Not knowing where I got the strength, I leapt to my feet and ran, sure though I was that I would soon be caught. But nobody bothered to chase me. I stumbled into a half-empty barrack hut and lay down on the floor. There was plenty of room.

But only till the marching column of prisoners arrived. The last of them reached the camp after darkness had fallen, and the huts became so crowded that there was not even room to sit down. The weaker prisoners were just crushed to death. Determined that this was not going to happen to me, I fought my way to the door, not caring where I trod. Indeed, I had no option but to walk and stumble over bodies, arms, legs and heads, the target of blows at every step, until I reached the open air.

Outside the darkness was Stygian, except for an occasional flash of lightning. Then came the thunder, and the rain began pouring down again. I groped my way to a tree trunk and lay down in the mud, my head against the fallen tree. It was so comfortable lying there. I had not had such a comfortable bed for more than a year. Now I could sleep all day long. Nobody bothered me, I felt no hunger, and there was no shortage of water. Every now and then, I filled myself up with mud and fell asleep again. Only once was I disturbed. A burial detail, taking me for dead, picked me up and prepared to carry me away. As soon as I showed signs of life, however, they let me fall again.

THE LIBERATION

On the fifth day, it was May 5, the rattle of machine-gun fire woke me up. It lasted for half an hour and then I heard cheering. All the prisoners streamed out of the barracks, and I asked one of them what had happened. 'Don't you know?' he asked in amazement. 'The Americans are here, we're free!'

I burst into tears and wept for a long time, until my head fell back onto my tree branch and I slept.

When I awoke—twenty-two days later—I was in the grip of a raging thirst. As usual, I bent my head downwards to slake it by lapping up some of the water from the mud I was lying in. But I was disappointed. My tongue met nothing but dryness. I lay back and opened my mouth wide in the hope of catching some of the rain that was still, as far as I knew, streaming down from the sky. Still nothing. Petulantly, I opened my eyes. At first I could not see anything very clearly. Everything swam hazily about me. But my sight cleared from second to second and within a few moments I could see everything.

I was dreaming, obviously, for I seemed to be

lying in bed between clean, white sheets. This must be some kind of Nazi trick. Every prisoner knew how dangerous it was when the S.S. behaved with propriety, when they showed a little humanity. I tried to raise my arms and discovered that my left arm was strapped to the bed. A long needle was stuck in it, and a thin tube ran from the needle to a bottle hanging neck-down some way away and above me. It was half full of some brownish fluid.

Now I knew what was happening. I was being given my 'squirts', as we called them in the concentration camps. Some of the more educated prisoners used to call them 'eternity injections', because the recipient went straight to eternity. The S.S., those masters of the euphemistic and concealing phrase, called them 'release or mercy injections'. A uniformed German soldier was standing at the foot of the bed. 'Don't worry,' he said reassuringly as my glance met his, 'you're free now, it is we who are the prisoners.' A typical Nazi joke, I thought to myself. They specialized in that kind of grisly humour. Then I saw another bed next to mine.

'Yes, it's true,' said the prisoner who was occupying it. 'We've been free for three weeks now.'

The soldier divined my thoughts. 'That is not a lethal injection, it's a blood transfusion.' Vaguely, I began to recall the prisoner who had shouted: 'The Americans are here!' But some doubt still lingered in my mind. At that moment, an American soldier appeared and distributed chocolate and sweets. My doubt vanished.

When I no longer needed any transfusions I was ready to get up, dress and go home. The doctor was horrified. 'Good God, man,' he exclaimed. 'You can't get up yet. You have to get better first.'

'What?' I said. 'In the concentration camp one had to be ill in order to survive, but now I don't have to be ill any more.'

'Well, you'll have to stay in bed for a few more days, and then you will be able to get up,' he replied. I did not know then that 'a few days' would drag on into years.

There was a temperature chart at the head of my bed, with a mass of Latin names I could not understand, except for two—typhus and tuberculosis. Instead of being discharged after a few days, I began coughing up blood from my lungs and had to have ice packs applied to my chest. But I took all this a great deal less seriously than the worried doctor. I could not believe that God would have helped me to survive the camps so miraculously only to let me die in hospital when it was all over.

254

The hospital was in Austria, at a place called Hörsching, near Wels. When it was closed down, the Americans moved me to a T.B. sanatorium at No. 6 Riesenhoftstrasse, in Linz-Urfahr. I stayed there until January, 1946, my condition gradually worsening all the time. There would seem to be some improvement, but it was always followed by a relapse.

In the meantime, I wrote letter after letter to my home village in an effort to find out if any of my family had come through the war and the camps alive. But to no avail. Nobody answered.

The doctors were all agreed that my case was hopeless, yet spring came and the other twenty-one patients in my ward all died, one by one, but I still lingered on. The sister, Sister Clara, was a devout and extraordinarily noble person, and she treated me as if I were her own child. Often, when she came back from church, she used to say to me: 'Bubi, I prayed for your recovery,' and once, when my situation was critical, she stayed up with me all night.

She used to try, delicately and tactfully, to convert me to her faith, which, so she said, would open a gate into paradise for my soul. I felt that she was speaking with deep religious conviction, so I was not brusque with her. 'Sister,' I said, 'I have not the

255

slightest intention of going to paradise yet. I want to stay here on earth a good long time.'

Some time later, I was transferred to a sanatorium at Goisern, in Upper Austria. For over a year now, I had had a high temperature. This and the lack of news of my family began slowly to sap my will to live. Day after day, I lay in bed with my eyes closed, not even wanting to eat. I had no desire to live any more, since all my family were dead. I told the senior doctor, Dr Weidinger, as much, when he asked me why I was letting myself go downhill.

I had hardly finished speaking, when a nurse rushed in with a telegram for me. I tore it open with shaking hands. Dated May 10, 1946, it said: 'Lili, Michael, Rifka and Father all well.'

'Praise be to God,' I cried, leaping out of bed.